TO:

Lynn & Jason

love & grace,

Michael Simone

1/13/13

ISAIAH
66:2

"I've done my fair share of flying—in the cockpit and as a

passenger. I know what it takes to keep a plane on course,

and it pales in comparison to navigating life and leadership.

In *Altitude*, Michael Simone calls serious minded

Christ-followers to step it up in several critical areas of life.

The practical wisdom in this book can impact

the trajectory of your life, if you let it."

Bill Hybels, Senior Pastor
Willow Creek Community Church
President, Board of Directors
Willow Creek Association

Altitude
by Michael Simone

© Copyright 2012 by Michael Simone

Edited by Paul Braoudakis

ISBN 978-1-938467-54-7

First Edition

Published by

210 60th Street, Virginia Beach, VA 23451
www.koehlerbooks.com
212-574-7939

In association with

Publisher
John Köehler

Executive Editor
Joe Coccaro

 In an effort to support local communities, raise awareness and funds, Morgan James Publishing donates a percentage of all book sales for the life of each book to Habitat for Humanity Peninsula and Greater Williamsburg.
Get involved today, visit www.MorganJamesBuilds.com

Contents

Acknowledgments

My heart is pounding with gratitude. Since 1971, so many friends have encouraged me to gain Altitude and make the strategic moves that are my flight. I thank all of you for wisdom, grace, and laughter. Through spills and chills, twists and turns, I'm truly *wealthy in my friends*. Those named here have been instrumental in making Altitude a gift to and from my heart.

John Koehler, my Lombardi

Paul Braoudakis, my editor and friend

Lynda Gorniewicz, my tireless Pastoral Assistant,
with a true servant's heart

Jo Ann Keller, my proofer and grammar police

David Stas and Millie Wiggs, for technical wizardry

Debbie Hudson, my Executive Administrator
and Cardinals fan

The Staff of Spring Branch, a team committed to excellence

The Elders and ministry leadership teams of Spring Branch,
you live out Proverbs 3:5-6

The Members and Friends of Spring Branch,
you do whatever it takes

Gene and Angie Loving, for dogs and rest

Bob Voogt, for hope and encouragement
(& front row seats at Yankee Stadium)

Henry and Luree Holt, for sharing the vision of this book

ORPHANetwork, a staff and board committed to
changing lives in Nicaragua

Bill, Jimmy, Nancy, Gary, Steve, Corinne, Greg,
Lisa, Aliece, Dave, Steven, Jean, Cindy and the
Willow Creek Association Staff, for Leadership Altitude

Ashley Simone, I love seeing everything you create

Travis Simone, I love hearing you teach biblical principles

Gail, the real story of Altitude is your heart
You create the future

To Gail

You move hearts with lights
You give life to moments of wonder
You pull down heaven's stars for children to play with
You paint the Great Mystery in breathless color
You fly with grace

Altitude

your next move changes everything

Letters From God & Small Group
Study Guide Included

Michael Simone

NEW YORK
VIRGINIA

Those who hope in the Lord
will renew their strength.
They will soar on wings like eagles.

Isaiah 40:31

Introduction

YOU FLY THROUGH life at the speed of life. Your velocity blurs the edges of cognition. The afterburners are always on. If you're like me there are a few things you're trying to fix or unravel while zooming along. Doing that is never easy. So, how's it going as you rip through reality?

Altitude is the concept I use to describe whether or not life is working. I know some parts of your life are working and some parts of your life are messy. I know because that's how mine is. Altitude ultimately comes down to two pithy questions. *Do you know who you are? Do you know where you're going?* That being established at the fragile beginning of this book, I also need to tell you one thought stuck fast in my mind—*"The best way to predict the future is to create it."* [1] Peter Drucker said it. I believe it. Another way to read Drucker's thought is, *your next move changes everything.* I believe that, too. Altitude is gained or lost from the sum of your moves, as you are answering two succinct questions. That statement tells the story of my life. It tells your story, too.

YOUR NEXT MOVE CHANGES EVERYTHING

Let me tell you how those five words flew into my brain one spring day. It was one of those perfect afternoons in April. No showers in sight. It was a grand day for an old ball game. I picked up my father-in-law and drove to Williamsburg, from Virginia Beach, for a JV baseball game. My son was playing center field. The obligatory bag of peanuts was ready to cast her wickery husks on the ground. For some reason there was a small bench down the right field line, as if built there just for us. With our rustic box seats and crunching away, we watched possibly the sloppiest baseball game in history. No one could catch a ball. No one knew what to do with the ball. The score went back and forth, forth and back. Mercifully, that last inning arrived. The score was 8-7 in favor of the home team. There were two outs when my son came up to bat. He smacked a fastball up the middle. The tying run aboard, our spirits soared in hope of extra innings.

Then I realized what we were up against. Our weakest hitter shuffled toward the plate. Bat loomed bigger than boy. I sniffed the air, now turning cool in the fading afternoon. *Trouble.* I frowned and set down the peanuts. The first pitch was a rocket. *Strike one!* My son stole second base. The next fastball, like a bat out of a bad place, was never seen by the batter. *Strike two!* My son stole third. Tension filled the air. Would the unthinkable happen, or would we suffer *the legendary agony of defeat?* These are the moments we live for in sports. The pitcher looked in. My son took a bold lead off third. The batter hunched over home base trying to get in touch with his inner Babe Ruth. The pitch zoomed. *"Pow,"* shrieked the catcher's mitt! *Strike three!*

Game over. I walked across the diamond toward my son who was walking toward me. He asked a question I'll never forget. *"How much did we lose by, Dad?"* Stopped in my tracks I responded, *"How much did we lose by? One run. You should've stolen home!"* I was stymied. He was in the game! He had a uniform on! He was on the team! But he didn't know what the score was! *His next move could have changed everything!*

Now, I don't know what would have happened if he had tried to steal home. He might have been out. He might have been safe. But I do know this. As he broke for home, old men would rise to their feet putting weathered hands over their hearts. Women holding babies would clutch them a little tighter, opening their mouths in astonishment. Kids playing behind the fence would stop pushing and throwing dirt to stare at this blur of red numbers, white pants, and silver cleats, racing toward doom or destiny. A magnificent slide! A billowing cloud of dust rising to heaven! *The umpire shouts*—and I don't know if he exclaims "Safe!" or "Out!" But I do know this—it would have been one heck of a finish to a baseball game!

Forty-two years ago, I made a move that changed everything. I was visiting a friend at Taylor University in Upland, Indiana. One bitter cold February night, after meeting with the football team for a Bible study, the first Bible study of my life, I walked back to the dorm pondering who I was and where I was going. I was just passing through Indiana on my quest to find the meaning of life. I was committed to travel the paved and rocky roads of the world to find an answer to the riddle of me. But I was ambushed in *hoosierland.* I was embraced by God on a clear, starry night. My move of asking Christ to change me that night was a 180 degree turnabout. I hadn't expected God to show up in my brain like a fiery lightning strike. I wasn't prepared for an epiphany. But He's been showing up ever since with amazing consistency.

So here I am, knowing that *your next move changes everything,* because I've lived it into my fifth decade of faith. I've seen a church sprout and grow out of the most confusing time in my life. I've seen an organization caring for orphans in Nicaragua explode from my heart. I've seen water, for a village in Togo, gush because of an unpredictable lunch with a friend in Copenhagen. And I've experienced daily the wonder, miracle, and mystery of what happens when you make the next move with Him.

Inside you'll find eight critical moves for creating your life. Air Traffic Control sections will help you land your plane. My hope is for you to grab or invent your next move. My prayer is for you to create your future. May you find out who you are and where you're going. May you gain Altitude all your days.

Michael Simone
Virginia Beach, Virginia

Your First Move

Desperately Seeking Altitude

I don't believe

for a second
that success is just about
self-motivation. If that were all it took,
all any of us would ever need is a little pep rally
now and again and we'd soar to the stars.
But after all the rah-rahs and the warm feelings
wear off, it's ultimately about action.
When you strap into your jet, you have to push up the
throttle and then release the brakes to take off.

Lt. Col. Rob "Waldo" Waldman
Never Fly Solo

YOU GET ON A PLANE. You get off a plane. You've adjusted to TSA screenings. You daydream as you get patted down. You log miles and collect points. You're moving your personal body system over oceans, mountain ranges, and the occasional metropolis. But with all the aerial gymnastics, questions float in the air. Who's flying your plane? Are you going anywhere significant? Are you desperately seeking Altitude?

We've grown up in a generation where something that was steeped in science fiction is now humdrum reality. We don't raise an eyebrow or look up as the flight attendant's rote safety announcements annoyingly interfere with our Kindle concentration (*I know my seat can float. I know to blow into the little tube thingy*). In our oblivion, we fail to appreciate the most startling of realities—we're in a can being hurtled through space at four times the average Daytona 500 speed.

PHYSICS LESSON

We fly by gaining support from the air, and we defy gravity by using static lift. We gain speed by increasing power (or thrust), which also determines Altitude. As we ascend, engines work more efficiently, we get where we are going faster, and we rise above the majority of turbulence.

So, why the physics lesson? Well, there's a lot of similarity between Altitude and relationships. We all ride the skies of relationships. Relationships take us up and bring us down. There are rumbling takeoffs and scary nosedives as we hope for safe landings in life. Altitude is all about getting the answers to your wobbly relational questions. And you have questions. We all do. Altitude is the way you live your life. You either keep learning and growing (thrust) and safely get to your destinations, or you find your flight has been canceled. You're grounded until conditions clear up. How long you're grounded might just be up to you.

Altitude has a spiritual altimeter and compass. One indicates the level of connectedness with God; the other gives you the coordinates of where life is taking you. Together, those readings tell the stories of your flights. There are times when we look at our instrument panel and it seems like a bunch of dials we can't make heads or tails of. If we're honest, we have to admit that our spiritual lives are oftentimes the same way. Who God is and where life is taking us can feel like a mystery.

So, let's take some flying lessons and explore the skies of your relationships. We all need to find out *who* is flying our plane. The future depends on it.

FLIGHT PLAN

It pays to take spiritual flying lessons. You'll be glad you did when it's foggy or when you come in for a landing and there's snow on the runway. Learn to fly right and you can even *set 'er down* on a patch of dirt if necessary. Some of us old-timers know there are a lot of potholed airstrips in the flight plan of life. There are creaky wings and landing gear bumpedy bumps, too. Most of the time you need all the help God can give, as you pray for safe relationship landings. Let's begin by looking at a man who thought he was an expert pilot but came up desperately seeking altitude. His name is Solomon. This is the story of his flight.

"Meaningless! Meaningless!"
  says the Teacher.
"Utterly meaningless!
  Everything is meaningless."
What does man gain from all his labor
  at which he toils under the sun?
Generations come and generations go,
  but the earth remains forever.
The sun rises and the sun sets,
  and hurries back to where it rises.
The wind blows to the south
  and turns to the north;
round and round it goes,
  ever returning on its course.
All streams flow into the sea,
  yet the sea is never full.
To the place the streams come from,
  there they return again.
All things are wearisome,
  more than one can say.
The eye never has enough of seeing,
  nor the ear its fill of hearing.
What has been will be again,
  what has been done will be done again;
there is nothing new under the sun.
  Is there anything of which one can say,
  "Look! This is something new"?

(Ecclesiastes 1:2-10)

So, Solomon, a brilliant guy, says, *Take a look around. Take a good look. Peel back the layers of life. Go ahead. There's nothing there. Trust me, I've looked at it. I've thought about it. I've gone through this over and over again in my mind. I wish it wasn't so, but life cannot pay off for you. It hasn't paid off for me. Life wears me out.*

"I have seen all the things that are done under the sun; all of them are meaningless, a chasing after the wind." (Ecclesiastes 1:14)

Then he gives the back story. He says in essence, *Let me show you how I got here.*

I thought in my heart, "Come now, I will test you with pleasure to find out what is good." But that also proved to be meaningless.

"Laughter," I said, "is foolish. And what does pleasure accomplish?" I tried cheering myself with wine, and embracing folly—my mind still guiding me with wisdom. I wanted to see what was worthwhile for men to do under heaven during the few days of their lives.

I undertook great projects: I built houses for myself and planted vineyards. I made gardens and parks and planted all kinds of fruit trees in them. I made reservoirs to water groves of flourishing trees. I bought male and female slaves and had other slaves who were born in my house. I also owned more herds and flocks than anyone in Jerusalem before me. I amassed silver and gold for myself, and the treasure of kings and provinces. I acquired men and women singers, and a harem as well—the delights of the heart of man. I became greater by far than anyone in Jerusalem before me. In all this my wisdom stayed with me.

I denied myself nothing my eyes desired; I refused my heart no pleasure.

My heart took delight in all my work, and this was the reward for all my labor. Yet when I surveyed all that my hands had done and what I had toiled to achieve, everything was meaningless, a chasing after the wind; nothing was gained under the sun.

(Ecclesiastes 2:1-11)

Solomon is desperate for Altitude. He's trying to gain it through pleasure. He's got *American Idol* and *The Voice* going on. He's got rodeos. He's got his own bank he can walk into any time he needs cash. He doesn't need a PIN. He signs and goes. He's trying to fly high through achievement, through production and by doing more. *Maybe if I create the highest buildings, the greatest structures, maybe I'll find something inside that feels like meaning and hope.* But it wasn't there. Zip. Nada.

In 2008, 4,000 books were published on happiness, while a mere 50 books on the topic were released in 2000. [1] Do you think there's a market out there for happiness? Do you think people are trying to figure this out? Thousands of years earlier, Solomon was writing his own book on happiness. You know what? It wasn't happy. His life screams at him, *Whatever you do, it will not pay off for you!* And so, in futility, he responds at the level of a deep inner ache.

So I hated life, because the work that is done under
the sun was grievous to me. All of it is meaningless, a
chasing after the wind. I hated all the things I had toiled
for under the sun, because I must leave them to the one
who comes after me. And who knows whether he will be
a wise man or a fool? Yet he will have control over all the
work into which I have poured my effort and skill under
the sun. This too is meaningless.
(Ecclesiastes 2:17-19)

I have sweat equity he argues with no one in particular.
*Then I pass it on to someone else? How do they know what to
do with what I've given them? How do I know I can really trust
anyone?* It looks like he's going under. But in the midst of it all,
he gets one glimmer of hope.

A man can do nothing better than to eat and drink
and find satisfaction in his work. This too, I can see is
from the hand of God, for without him who can eat or
find enjoyment? (Ecclesiastes 2:24)

A shot of wind beneath his wings! He gains some Altitude. As
he's trying to fill up something on the inside that's insatiable, he
thinks, *Wait a minute! Maybe I'm onto something here. Maybe
it's about more than the latest stuff, the latest acquisitions, or
the latest indulgences. Maybe it's about squeezing the life God
has given me, while enjoying God in the process! Planning great
times with friends and family is one way to gain Altitude. Think
weddings. Think ball games. Think concerts. Think celebrations.*

Solomon comes up with two **Summary Statements.** Here's the first.

> I have seen something else under the sun: The race is not to the swift or the battle to the strong, nor does food come to the wise or wealth to the brilliant or favor to the learned; but time and chance happen to them all. (Ecclesiastes 9:11)

He's essentially saying, *Let me tell you something. I've looked at all this stuff. Life isn't fair. You have expectations that may not be met. You have plans. They may go south. You have ideas about the way you want things to be, but it might not work that way for you. You can't control anything. Stay flexible.*

Here's the second. He wraps up all the loose ends of his angst as he has now risen to an Altitude that allows him to see his entire life unobstructed from 30,000 feet.

> Now all has been heard; here is the conclusion of the matter: Fear God and keep his commandments, for this is the whole duty of man. For God will bring every deed into judgment, including every hidden thing, whether it is good or evil. (Ecclesiastes 12:13-14)

What was Solomon desperate for? He was ultimately yearning for something to fill him up after he discovered he had the wrong set of expectations. He came face to face with the realization that stuff doesn't cut it. He needed something that eluded his grasp of power. Something that transcended him. Something intangible to his desires. That's when it hit him. The intangible was the tangible.

SPIRITUAL CALIBRATION

I think we all relate to his level of desperation. The frenzied global system is a hint. It's not just happening to a wise, rich king. It's happening to people all around the world who aren't spiritually calibrated. Even an airplane's most sophisticated instrumentation can become useless if it isn't calibrated. Compasses and GPS units become ineffective if they are not tuned to True North.

On July 16, 1999, we tragically lost yet another member of the Kennedy family as John F. Kennedy, Jr.'s self-piloted aircraft crashed into the ocean. After many months of investigation, official word came from the National Transportation Safety Board: The cause of the crash was "spatial disorientation." By definition, this is "the inability to correctly interpret aircraft altitude or airspeed in relation to the Earth or point of reference." John lost his bearings and didn't know where the horizon was. We agonize over misinterpreted points of reference. In the case

We agonize over misinterpreted points of reference. Spiritual calibration is a prerequisite for your earthly flight.

of our moral and spiritual Altitude, the horizon—the point of reference—is God. When we incorrectly interpret our Altitude without Him as our reference point, we become spatially disoriented. Spiritual calibration is a prerequisite for your earthly flight.

PILOT ERRORS

Statistics tell us that pilot error is the cause of most crashes. There are three major flying errors most people make.

The first one is when we try to fly high for short-term gains. Short-term gains are always about *What's in this for me? What does this mean for me? What am I going to get?* We need, instead, to understand how life is so much bigger than that. Finding ways to take care of people through long range planning and vision, over years and decades, is always the right move. God wants so much more from your life than you can imagine. Living for short term gains is like existing in a purgatory of middle school forever. I bet you know someone like that. Want to go back to being that cool? I didn't think so.

We also lose Altitude trying to fly the skies of impressing others. We marvel at our air show. *Look how high I flew! Look what I accomplished. Look at all the stuff I command. I have a runway with my name on it.* Achievement for the right reasons is good, but when it's rooted in self-serving moves, it lacks moral integrity. Trust in the words of a much wiser king. He found a self-congratulatory victory dance masks aimless wandering—or deep thirst for the *intangible tangible.*

Another error we make is we try to fly high in order to run away from something, someone, or even ourselves. We try to go higher and higher, hoping jet stream Altitude will give us distance from our pervasive problem. We can never run away from problems whether our thrust is forward or our lift vertical. We quirkily try to deny things we need to change and work on. Essentially we end up going nowhere. We fly by the seat of our jeans into nebulous skies. Running, gunning, and denying never gain Altitude for the demands of life.

ALTITUDE UNPACKED

• I believe you can have better relationships

• I believe you have blind spots in relationships

• I believe relationships that are stuck can get unstuck

• I believe there are some relationships that are never
  going to work and that wasn't a choice you made, but
  it's a choice you must accept at times

• I believe you need to learn more about how
  you sometimes set yourself up for difficulties in
  relationships

• I believe you're responsible for your own relational
  maturity

• I believe you need God in all of your relationships

• I believe God must be the primary relationship of
  your life

WHO OWNS YOUR PLANE?

I believe we can have better relationships. I believe relationships that are stuck can get unstuck. I believe there are some relationships that are never going to work. It wasn't necessarily because of a choice we made, but it's a choice we must accept at times. But I also believe we need to learn more about how we sometimes set ourselves up for difficulties in relationships. Sometimes we just keep doing the same thing over and over and we wonder why we're at the same place. The truth is we set ourselves up for continuing problems. We see abundant examples of this in the news and, more often than not, we see it in our own lives. We are ultimately responsible for our own relational maturity and spiritual growth.

I recently attended an Ultimate Leadership workshop (cloudtownsend.com), where I spent five days looking at issues of spiritual and relational maturity. I crunched time for this into my schedule, because it's up to me to invest in becoming a better me.

Whether you're the Wright brothers, Amelia Earhart, Chuck Yeager, John Glenn, Sally Ride, or Felix Baumgartner, to gain the kind of Altitude that satisfies your desperate longings for life and fills your heart with substance, you need a solid flight plan. Here are some Altitude thoughts to ponder.

First, you must decide who owns your plane. That's what Solomon was trying to ascertain. Who owns your life? Who are you ultimately responsible to? Is it you, your parents, your boss, your friends, or God? Who owns your aircraft? You must also decide you can't fly by the seat of your pants anymore. You've been doing the same old things and expecting different results out of your relationships. Are they really going to get better and deeper on their own? You've got to get out of the holding pattern you're in. And in order to do that, you must decide who owns your life?

Next, as unnatural as it may feel at first, you must also decide to fly a mission that will fail without God in it. Put yourself out there on the edge and say, *God, right now I'm taking this flight, but I know without You I'm going down.* You've *got* to go there. You've got to go there relationally *for* Him and *with* Him and see what He does. Your mission might be starting a new career, finding a non-profit to volunteer with, solving a complex problem at work, or finally going on that mission trip. *You must fly a mission that will fail without God in it. What's stirring inside you right now? That stirring is a clue to your unique mission. Your passion is your boarding pass.*

After college my heart was stirred to help young men in the inner city. Fast-forward to a job as Director of Youth Guidance, working with first time juvenile court referrals, in Paterson, New Jersey. I walked the streets with young men helping them find spiritual Altitude to change their lives. I still remember the effervescent Bleeker brothers and a socially marginalized kid named Bo, who lived over a bar. I took them on retreats. I took them to experience Rahway State Prison. I invited a New York Giant running back to play football with us. We were creating the future as they found out who they were and where they were going.

Finally, you must decide to teach someone else to fly. This is a requisite component of gaining spiritual Altitude—it's a vital component of every relationship. One way to achieve this is to invite someone into the spiritual flight plan you have found. There's another aspect to this, too. Once you have been flying for awhile and you've gained some Altitude, you have a deep responsibility to mentor a new "pilot" regarding trouble spots. Pilots routinely radio in bad weather and turbulence to the towers so they can warn other pilots. As we gain Altitude, we have that same obligation to those who are new to the flight plan.

Here's an example of teaching others to fly from an F-16 fighter pilot.

> "I embraced the phrase 'Push it up!' and carried it with me into my professional life. It has become a metaphor for taking fierce action for my personal mission and my team's mission. I encourage you to use it, too, because those three short words symbolize everything it takes to step onto—the path to victory. It stands for maximum trust and maximum effort. It is the thrust that rockets you forward on the runway and into the air with confidence that you can fly, fight, and win." [2]

PUSH IT UP

Not long ago, I went to a memorial service for a good friend of mine who passed away at 89. He changed my life when I didn't even know it was changing. He was a leader, a father, a husband, and a grandfather. Regardless of how busy this naturally made him, every time I went to him with a problem, he made time for me. He let me sit there pouring out my inexperience and immaturity, and then he would say, "Michael, we're going to look at this the way God would look at it. We're going to remember ancient wisdom. Let me tell you this story from my life." I didn't realize it, but every time I went to him he just made time for me.

He changed my life because he made time to teach me how to *push it up*.

During the eulogy at his memorial service, many talked about his character and ministry. He was the first Greek Orthodox chaplain in the United States Navy. He touched lives all over the world. But he gave me a special set of gifts. He gave me his transparency and vulnerability. He opened up to me about his failures. He gave me fierce flying lessons.

Pushing it up gives us lift and raises our Altitude. We must decide who owns our plane. We have to decide to fly a mission that will fail without Him. And we must teach others how to fly.

THE POWER QUESTION

You never gain Altitude without power. The more Altitude you want, the more power you must harness. One crucial question remains. *Where do you get power for your next move?* We'll look at that concept from various angles in the chapters ahead. Solomon uncovered the Power. It's the first lesson of flight. And as I put together the words and thoughts that would eventually become this chapter, the Power showed up and wrote me a letter.

I believe it's written for you too.

Dear Michael,

In the beginning, I created what you call Altitude. I created relationship because it is the only way I have ever known Myself. I am relationship. I live in relationship. I nurture relationship. I teach truth relationally. All truth is relational because truth is who I am. You think truth is a moral compass you follow, but truth is the power of life in raw form. Without that power you won't gain relational Altitude.

The greatest power to create comes from relationship. The greatest power to destroy also comes from relationship. Therefore, connecting to Me is the only way you will survive. Without Me being in you and without you being driven by My Spirit, there's nothing. There is no Altitude where there is no real power. There may be posing, posturing, impostering, and finally imploding, but climbing the skies of relationships takes power...lots of it.

I am the Power. So, my first flying lesson is to advise you that without Me you can't even get off the ground to dust crops. All of your attempts at flight will end up with sputtering engines and tipsy takeoffs if you call out to Me with your lips but not your heart. It is with My heart in your heart that relationships find the air. In trusting the Spirit's wings, your life soars.

Even when I allow you to be grounded for the sake of teaching you more about flying, it is My heart that is always ready to take you to new heights again. And as you will learn, those heights are not just for the spectacular view or to give you joy. They are so you can see how much this world is still hurting and how desperately it needs us to teach them fierce flying lessons, too. Yes, you read that correctly. I did say "us." With Me it has always been about a relationship with you. I have longed to fly with you since before the world began. With My wings you will go where you currently have no strength to go. You'll land on runways of confusion and suffering and we will bring the flight plan of love and grace to many. We will teach truth and people will learn to fly. One day I will bring you to a place where you will know flying in a way that's impossible to describe to you now.

Remember this, to fly in this world is to first see relationships with My eyes and heart. That's what My Son taught you when He talked about being born from above. He was giving you that first flying lesson. That was, always has been, and always will be, all the Altitude you need for your flight home.

Pushing it up...with you,

Air Traffic Control

1. How does the intangible become the tangible in your pursuit of Altitude?
(Review Ecclesiastes 12:13-14)

2. When you look at the Altitude Unpacked list, which statement(s) connects to your heart right now?

_____

_____

_____

_____

3. Who owns your plane? Parents? Work? Financial stress? God? Which two are most in tension?

_____

_____

_____

_____

4. What's stirring in your heart? Is there a mission you are planning to fly? Describe it to the group. What are the challenges? How do you need to see God show up?

_____

_____

_____

_____

5. Who are you teaching to fly? What does that relationship mean to you?

_____

_____

_____

6. Who taught you to fly? What's a lesson you'll never forget?

_____

_____

_____

_____

Flying Higher

9 Things You Simply Must Do to Succeed in Love and Life, Dr. Henry Cloud (Thomas Nelson)

11 Indispensable Relationships You Can't Be Without, Leonard Sweet (David C. Cook)

Talent is Never Enough, John Maxwell (Thomas Nelson)

Uprising: A Revolution of the Soul, Erwin McManus (Thomas Nelson)

Fully Alive: Lighten Up and Live A Journey that Will Change Your Life, Ken Davis (Thomas Nelson)

Divine Alignment: How GodWink Moments Guide Your Spiritual Journey, SQuire Rushnell (Howard Books)

It's About Time!: 10 Smart Strategies to Avoid Time Traps and Invest Yourself Where It Matters, Carolyn Castleberry (Howard Books)

Bittersweet: Thoughts on Change, Grace, and Learning the Hard Way, Shauna Niequist (Zondervan)

Flight Log

My notes on Desperately Seeking Altitude

_____

_____

_____

_____

_____

_____

_____

_____

_____

_____

_____

_____

_____

_____

_____

_____

_____

_____

_____

_____

_____

_____

Your Second Move

Forgiveness is a Dirty Word

I believe

that what many of us are searching for
is not simply another message reassuring
us that God forgives freely.
As wonderful as it is, that information alone
is not enough to enable people to grow in their
experience of God's liberating forgiveness.
Many of us struggle at this point—not so much
with understanding the message of forgiveness,
but with living the reality of it.

John Ortberg
The Life You've Always Wanted

IN THE PAST FEW DAYS I've heard people say weird things. I've listened to bursts of tears during painful phone calls. I've been demanding of sales reps and I've been angry about way out in left field emails. Let's just say it and get it out of the way. Relationships are more like an NFL training camp than the warm, fuzzy, endearing images we see in our culture. Think *Survivor* not *Rachel Ray*. Think *Biggest Loser* weight room yelling not evocative *Apple* commercials. The business of maintaining, nurturing, and shaping relationships is arguably the hardest work you'll ever do.

One of the reasons you'll shed blood, sweat and tears is that forgiveness will wrangle itself into holiday, boardroom, and locker room moments. Baseball great Yogi Berra needed it. Hewlett Packard CEO Carly Fiorina had to utilize it when she least expected it. [1] Tiger Woods called us into a sobering national conversation about it. In our lifetime, we've seen public apologies or pleas for forgiveness from baseball players, an NFL quarterback, Olympians, assorted politicians, and financial wizards. Wait a few minutes and somebody you know will be asking you to pardon them.

In my sixth decade of life, without a doubt, one of the most stressful and tedious parts of my journey has to do with forgiveness. Almost every cotton-pickin' day, from grocery store impatience to meeting discombobulations, to things I say that simply didn't come out right, I come away having to forgive something or someone about something.

How about you? How many times did you have to forgive someone last week? How many times did you need to be forgiven? How many times did you ask God to forgive *you*? How many times did you forget to ask God to forgive you, but you want to catch up right now? How much of your stress is coming from relational issues that are unresolved inside your heart and head?

DON'T LET YESTERDAY USE UP TODAY

Forgiveness is a tough issue because it involves a ton of emotion, and emotions can be slippery. Forgiveness can bind us in a taut psychological thriller of relational deceit. Our lives can become seedbeds of bewilderment as we teeter between hanging on and letting go. Letting go is a tougher-than-anyone-would-think issue, because discerning what to forgive and what not to forgive can be confusing. Forgiveness is agonizing in another way. You might forgive but can you *truly forget* and get past the hurt?

"Don't let yesterday use up too much of today." [2] This famous proverb echoes through the decades. It stings us with truth. *"Don't let yesterday use up too much of today."* Without understanding forgiveness, at best your life may be mildly stressful, at worst your nights might crush the life out of you. Lewis Smedes, a renowned Christian author, ethicist, and theologian, would say that without forgiveness you'll be a prisoner in your own mind. Shakespeare put it eloquently when he penned, *"Who from crimes would pardoned be, in mercy should set others free."* [3]

But the words that best mine the caverns of forgiveness are radical and personal.

"For if you forgive men when they sin against you, your heavenly Father will also forgive you. But if you do not forgive men their sins, your father will not forgive your sins." (Matthew 6:14-15)

If you're anything like me, when you first read that, you're probably shouting back in your mind: *Come on! Why'd you make it that hard? You don't know the people I'm dealing with down here! My life is like one painfully long episode of The Office! What about all that forgiveness is free and grace stuff?!* [4] *Now there are conditions? You're making me work too hard!*

WHAT GOD WANTS

Here's the deal. God wants us to act like He acts. He encourages us to do just that. You need to forgive to show God you get it. It's not supposed to be theologically logical. In fact, the longer you're alive, the more you'll find those two words—*theologically logical* — aren't logical. Let's keep rolling and zoom in on Peter.

"Then Peter came to Jesus and asked, "Lord, how many times shall I forgive my brother when he sins against me? Up to seven times?" (Matthew 18:21)

Peter thought this was a magnanimous move. He thought he would clean up on Double Jeopardy with his answer in the form of a question. Cut to the back story. The culture was replete with discussions about forgiveness. Experts on relational chaos came up with a system by which you had to forgive three times. A fourth time was out of the question. The formula was three times—forgiveness works. Then if somebody keeps getting in your face, you shut them down. It's neat. It's clean. You've done everything you can possibly do. You went the limit. You worked the formula. You're going to sleep like a baby.

Get ready to hear a big bubble pop. Jesus stunned all in attendance when He answered,

> "I tell you, not seven times, but seventy-seven times." (Matthew 18:22) In some translations it says seventy times seven—490 times? Really? Nary a number can contain it. There's an attitude here. There's a profound understanding here. Forgiveness is never going to end. Forgiveness is a marathon. The only way to live life is to forgive life. The only way to get through life is to give up our rule book on fairness. You're going to have to get your hands dirty to do this. You're going to have to get knee-deep in the relational muck and mire. *Forgiveness is a dirty word.*

MORAL INVENTORY

From David, we get two other views of forgiveness.

> "The sacrifices of God are a broken spirit; a broken and contrite heart, O God, you will not despise [turn away from]." (Psalm 51:17)

This is where David woke up to something extremely important in terms of bringing faith and life together. The inception of forgiveness is when you're broken and know you need to be forgiven. Forgiveness begins with a shattered heart—a heart that agonizes over having failed someone. That's the forgiveness power switch. God never turns away from gut-level honesty. Finding your brokenness brings you face to face with God. Taking a long hard look at your own failures is a good research project. That's why taking Step 4 in a recovery program is such a crucial step. This step requires a person to make a searching and fearless moral inventory. That's why asking yourself some hard questions is crucial. *Why do I always have to be right? Why did I get angry right after church? What did I do to contribute to that relational debacle?*

"Forgive my hidden faults." (Psalm 19:12)

That's a heady concept for a mature person. This person admits, *Even when I'm doing good, even when I think I'm getting my act together, I probably still need to be forgiven for some attitudinal freight. What about things I'm not doing that I should see and do? What about ways I'm not thinking that I should be thinking? I need God to forgive my hidden peccadillos. I need His view on stuff that trips me up in the recesses of my mind.* Forgiveness is multi-directional. It always gets to the heart of our clandestine motivations. God is actively looking for that type of person. He's vigorously seeking out—

"The one who is humble and contrite in spirit and trembles at my word." (Isaiah 66:2)

This is where faith and life collide. God has forever had an idea of the kind of person He is looking for. The obvious questions stealthily tracking you now are—

Am I that person? Do I want to be?

You can be.

FIVE TYPES OF FORGIVENESS

From my vantage point, there are at least five types of forgiveness. You need to understand the five types to know *how* to forgive, to know *when* to forgive, to know *who* should be forgiven and *what* the presuppositions of that forgiveness are.

Reset Button Forgiveness

I may have inadvertently invented this form of forgiveness from my own personal failures. I call this relational move *reset button forgiveness*. The name comes from a smaller-than-a-dime red button on the back of my dad's massive RCA Victor stereo. This 1962 granddaddy of the iPod was a gargantuan piece of furniture that took up most of our living room. You'd need a forklift to move it. Whenever the stereo stegosaurus refused to crank out the tunes, I leaned over the massive frame, reached the magic red button in the back, and gently pushed. Voilà! All was well in Musicland again, and the sounds of Julius Larosa, Mantovani, and Herb Alpert wafted through our home.

I learned reset button forgiveness early in my marriage— because I was wrong a lot. Something I did would stop the music. It wasn't only because my discerning wife told me so! I just stumbled into *I'm really wrong a lot* as a sad, albeit prevalent, truth of my existence. But since I hold fast to the gridiron maxim that the best offense is a good defense, why choose to lead with humility right from the line of scrimmage? Why risk being humble and contrite when you can be even more humble and contrite later?

So, here's what going on offense looked like for me. I would deftly manipulate my wife to think like I wanted her to think, act like I wanted her to act, and talk like I wanted her to talk. My strategy was to take over her mind with love and grace. In my despotic little cranial zone I would think, *I'm so smooth, she doesn't even know she's being boondoggled!* It was the ultimate Jedi mind trick.

I would try to get her to rubber-stamp things. I would put the stamp in her hand and move her arm. I'd say *thank you* for agreeing with me about all these great decisions I'm making (these are the machinations of a very lost person). *But she wouldn't let me live out my lost-ness.* God gave me a wife who was gracious enough not only to want to see me grow, but who was willing to ride out some crazy days in the process. I don't understand how someone could want to do that for almost four decades. Therein was born reset button forgiveness.

When I figured out I was manipulating the truth and trying to get her to be what I wanted her to be, I would proffer, "Can we push the reset button, go back, and start all over again?" Astonishingly, she would say, "Yes."

Amazing grace, how sweet the sound.

Suddenly, there appeared out of thin air a clean slate inviting me to live again. I love the reset button. It's better than an Easy Button. It's a great way to forgive. It's a great way to restore relationships. It ties into what Jesus was saying to Peter: "Seventy-seven times." It never ends. There's a mandate to constantly forgive. Resetting is the easiest way to get through all the little things that get in the way, when they're not that big and they're not that terrible, but they're just there gumming up the works. Try this theological invention of mine today. Some of you should've tried it before you read this chapter. It would've worked. You'll see that you'll get through a lot of little stuff a lot faster. There should be an app for this.

Faith Forgiveness

I was pulling out of a 7-11 parking lot one day and the light was red, so I was at the mercy of an unknown driver to let me into traffic. Let me set the scene. There was a van directly in front of me with barely enough space for me to pull out, but in my world there was room for a Mack truck. That's when the psychological game began.

I'm looking at Mr. Conversion Van Guy and he sort of notices I'm there, but he doesn't want to look at me. I'm staring at him but he's ignoring me. I'm thinking maybe he's gonna be nice. He's gonna let me go. The light's gonna turn in three... two... one seconds. He starts to inch forward, I start to inch forward. I look at him—he doesn't look at me—the light screams GREEN! Mr. Conversion Van Guy blows by me, tires screeching, fenders quaking, and then a whole bunch of cars blow by me. He wouldn't give me the space! But there was one final insult. As he left me in his dust, I glimpsed a shiny icon on the bumper... *a plastic fish!* The ubiquitous symbol of *I'm a Christian and I'm out here on the highways and byways ready to be a good samaritan!* I was mad! But I had to forgive on the basis of faith. I had to believe that God has a bigger vision than plastic fish deception. Faith forgiveness is based on God's character. It's not based upon shifting feelings. It doesn't work that way. It's God's way of acting. Besides, maybe the van was stolen.

> *Faith forgiveness is based on God's character. It's not shifting feelings. It doesn't work that way.*

A long time ago, Paul wrote—

"And we know that in all things God works for the good of those who love him, who have been called according to his purpose." (Romans 8:28)

When you believe that and live in that reality, you're able to live out faith forgiveness. This is the kind of forgiveness that says, *I don't feel like forgiving this and I don't even want to forgive this, but I believe God is better at working everything out than I am. I believe God's going to get it all sorted out at some point. Whatever happens might get sorted out next week, or it might get sorted out in eternity. It's not meant for me to worry about.* When you exercise faith forgiveness it's not about feelings and it's not about pushing the reset button. Sometimes you just have to say, "God, I'm going to trust that You have a bigger vision, a bigger plan, and I'm going to go with You on this one."

Faith forgiveness works in failed business deals. Faith forgiveness works in an unexpected job loss. Faith forgiveness even works when a spouse walks away. You can look back over the years and see the amazing results of faith forgiveness. You'll see what God did and how God loved you through what wasn't good, and how He turned you toward good. There's a place in your life right now needing faith forgiveness.

I still think the van was stolen.

Process Forgiveness

Process forgiveness happens over a lengthy amount of time. It's when you engage someone at a level of deep hurt, and over time you work on it until you get to a place where the relationship is stronger than it was before it was torn apart.

Tony Blair states it well:

"Realize that for both sides resolving the conflict is a journey, a process, not an event. Each side takes time to leave the past behind. A conflict is not simply a disagreement characterized by violence. It has a history and it creates a culture, with traditions, rituals and doctrine. It has a mind and a soul as well as a body. It is enduring, and it is deep." [5]

Imagine two sisters arguing over issues related to the impending death of their mother after a decade of descent into Alzheimer's. Decisions abound. Heels are dug in. Old wounds open. A funeral must be planned. A lifetime of business must be settled. Closets must be sorted through and new ownership must be established. How do you split a wedding ring? A wedding album? Feelings are hurt and communication is strained. They will need a process at some point. Forgiveness can't happen overnight in the hospital. It doesn't happen naturally just because their beloved mother is dying. It may take months, maybe years. It might take family meetings. It will take coffee and long walks and counseling. And, maybe, if they're willing to enter the process, they'll come out on the other side better knit together than ever before.

I knew two leaders who worked closely together for a long time. Then their relationship disintegrated overnight. They didn't talk for years. One day one of those men wrote a letter to the other detailing his frustrations. A phone call answered the letter. A lunch was set. They talked. They heard each other's hearts. It was a process. They kept talking. After so much brokenness, after so much heartache, these two leaders reinvented a relationship that is better today than it ever was. They were willing to enter a process with hope for something more. They even worked together again years later.

The process of forgiveness works, but you have to be willing to walk through buckets of hurt. You have to be willing to walk through years of not being on the same page with someone with whom you once had similar goals. But if you keep walking, there's a power and depth to forgiveness you'll never acquire by using a reset button or faith.

I know. I was one of those two leaders.

Boundary Forgiveness

Henry Cloud and John Townsend wrote in their best-selling book, *Boundaries Face to Face:*

"I know I'm supposed to forgive," a woman at a recent seminar said, "but I just can't open myself up to that kind of hurt anymore. I know I should forgive him and trust him, but if I let him back in the same thing will happen and I can't go through that again."

"Who said anything about trusting him?" I asked. "I don't think you should trust him, either."

"But you said I was supposed to forgive him? And if

I do that, doesn't that mean giving him another chance? Don't I have to open up again?"

"No you don't. Forgiveness and trust are two totally different things. In fact, that's part of your problem. Every time he's done this he's come back and apologized and you have just accepted him right back into your life and nothing has changed. You trusted him. Nothing was different. And he did it again. I don't think that's wise."

"Well," she asked, "how can I forgive him without opening myself up to being hurt again?"

"Good question.

We hear this problem over and over again. People have been hurt and they do one of two things. Either they confront the other person about something that has happened and the other person says he's sorry and they forgive, opening themselves up again and blindly trusting, or in fear of opening themselves up again they avoid the conversation and hold onto the hurt, fearing that forgiveness will make them vulnerable once again.

How do you resolve this dilemma?" [6]

You resolve it with boundary forgiveness. The past is what we look at when it comes to forgiveness. When something hurtful has been done to us, we need to figure out a way to let it go, and we need to figure out what we do with that hurt.

In 1980, President Jimmy Carter was going toe to toe with Ronald Reagan and they were all set for a momentous debate. But as Carter went to prepare, he realized his brief for the debate had been stolen. The other side had it. They would be able to prepare knowing full well what positions he was going to attack and what he was going to say. He had even crafted phrases he would memorize and use in the debate. They had all that information and took him down. Ronald Reagan was our president for the next eight years.

Carter was bitter. He went back to his life in Plains, Georgia, where he taught Sunday School every weekend. Two years passed since his presidency came to an end. He was still angry and bitter that his debate brief had been stolen. One day as he went to prepare his Sunday School lesson, he noticed a weighty topic. It hit him like a ton of political bricks. How could he go into church and teach about forgiveness when he was harboring bitterness and resentment towards the man who stole his playbook? He knew who the man was and, with steely resolve, he decided to finally do something about it.

Carter remembered the man had authored some books, and one of the books was about baseball. He went to a used bookstore and found a copy of it for a dollar. He bought it, read it, and actually loved the book. He then wrote a note to the author/thief, telling him how much he liked the book and that it only cost him a dollar (Yes, that was an intentional zing. We're not perfect, even when we're forgiving!). But in doing that, in appreciating this man's work, in contacting him in that way, Carter was able to let it go. The man wrote him back and it was over. It was done. [7]

That's why it says:

"Forgive us our debts as we have forgiven our debtors," (Matthew 6:12)

While it says in Luke 11:4:

"Forgive us our sins for we also forgive everyone who sins against us."

There are things in the past we have to let go of. The prayer Jesus gave His disciples has become one of the most famous prayers ever recorded. His prayer talks about this kind of forgiveness. While relational trust cannot always be restored, you can still forgive. You do that by putting a boundary on the past.

Jesus is quoted as saying:

"Do not give dogs what is sacred, do not throw your pearls to pigs." (Matthew 7:6)

Another translation says:

"Do not give what is holy to the dogs; nor cast your pearls before swine, lest they trample them under their feet, and turn and tear you to pieces."
(New King James Version)

This is where the Bible takes on boundary forgiveness. There's a time to forgive what someone did to you years ago, but there may not be enough trust to have anything but a very minimal relationship with this person. There are times when it's appropriate that the relationship has ended; when you have shown forgiveness but the relationship is no more. That's where the factor of trust comes into our understanding about forgiveness.

When trust is broken and can't be glued together, boundary forgiveness is the right option. Divorce? Business partner fallout? Friendship betrayal? Boundary forgiveness applies. Boundary forgiveness works. Make a move on a boundary.

Solo Forgiveness

Forgiving yourself for things you may be responsible for (or that were foisted upon you by others) is something you can't do cheaply or on the fly. You don't want to be caught in the net of the *blaming yourself game.* Solo forgiveness is *forgiving yourself.* It's forgiving you for being an imperfect you. M. Scott Peck, the psychiatrist who wrote *The Road Less Traveled*, has an updated version of that book called *Further Along the Road Less Traveled.* Within that book, he stated that, "The Blaming Game could also be called the, 'If It Weren't for You' game. Most of us have played it. There is a kind of circular, repetitive quality to this game that is hard to interrupt. Therefore, the only way to stop a game is to stop. That sounds simple, but in fact it is extremely difficult. Just how do you stop? Stopping the blaming game is called forgiveness. That is precisely what forgiveness is: the process of stopping, of ending, the Blaming Game. And it is tough." Sometimes you play the blaming game with yourself and you have to stop it. Don't get caught in a whitewash absolution move Peck would call *cheap forgiveness.* [8]

Cheap forgiveness is not the way to forgive yourself. It's superficial. All it does is hide the truth. Real forgiveness deals with what happened. Real forgiveness deals with the injustice. Real forgiveness deals with your own brokenness and the fact that you did something you shouldn't have done, thought something you shouldn't have thought, or said something you shouldn't have said. When you finally forgive yourself, you become freer than you ever could have been using cheap forgiveness.

Forgiving yourself is one of the most important works of our relational lives. What do you need to forgive yourself for? Something you did when you were a teenager or young adult? You can't go back and do it over. You can't press the reset button. But you can do solo forgiveness on it. You need to forgive and go on so you can be what God needs you to be today instead of wasting the energy of today on regrets of yesterday. *Don't let yesterday use up too much of today.*

Talking about forgiveness, Peck summarizes, *"The reason to forgive others is not for their sake, the reason to forgive is for our own sake."* [9] That applies to solo forgiveness, too. The reason to forgive is so we can be free and not have to deal with that stuff anymore. Solo forgiveness. You gotta do it. Boundary forgiveness. Sometimes you gotta forgive and walk away. Process forgiveness...it takes time. Reset Button forgiving is when we fail each other so we can quickly start living again. Faith forgiveness lets God guide the moment.

Forgiveness is a dirty word means you have to do something. You already know the name of the person you need reconciliation with. There's someone you need to go to and say you're sorry, or someone you need to engage with because there's something broken between you. Maybe you're not ready yet. Sometimes that's the way it is. But there comes a time when you *have* to do something. Now you have some options, as you get knee deep in the relational muck and mire.

Make your move to forgive. You will gain Altitude.

Dear Michael,

Once upon a creation, My image-bearers needed forgiveness, but they didn't know which way to go. Why do you hold onto so much pain in relationships? When you hold onto something, because somebody hurt you, you handcuff yourself. Opening up your heart to Me is the beginning of living a life that goes from stockpiling frustrations to setting a prisoner free. Remember not to base forgiveness on feelings. Feelings wax and wane. Your feelings need disciplined management most of the time. Part of getting your feelings under control is having faith that I know how to handle things. Everything will get sorted out sooner or later. I know you want sooner. But later is often a better choice. Maturity comes with later. Wisdom comes with later. Perseverance comes with later. Power comes with later.

Work on those reset buttons. Ask Me to help you forgive something in the past. Don't ever settle for cheap, superficial forgiveness. It looks clean and shiny at first, but disintegrates upon touch. True forgiveness is always somewhat dirty. I know because of My time with you. The cross is the harbinger of lasting relationships. My suffering was the messenger of an expensive contractual agreement. I paid all I had for you. On a craggy hill, I forgave your trespasses against Me. I signed the promise with My life. I announced forgiveness in the most horrible of moments. With dirty hands, I drew up the contract of freedom. Now, in all of your days, be My hands and feet. Go and do. Let everyone know the offer of freedom is secured by an exquisite, stunning, abundant grace which will transport your heart to eternity someday.

Once upon a creation a very dirty forgiveness shines like a streaking comet in the heavens. That's Me, up on the hill, pointing the way to your next move.

490 times works,

God

Air Traffic Control

1. Which type(s) of forgiveness do you most need to use this week?

      ☐ Reset Button Forgiveness

      ☐ Faith Forgiveness

      ☐ Process Forgiveness

      ☐ Boundary Forgiveness

      ☐ Solo Forgiveness

2. What's the hardest type for you to get a grip on?

_____

_____

_____

_____

_____

3. When you think about having a hidden fault what comes to mind?

_____

_____

_____

_____

4. Process forgiveness lasts the longest. How have you seen that process in your family or church relationships?

_____

_____

_____

_____

5. When have you been tempted to use cheap forgiveness?

_____

_____

_____

Optional

6. I need to forgive myself for_____

_____

_____

7. Talk about your solo forgiveness with a trusted friend or counselor.

Flying Higher

Forgive and Forget: Healing the Hurts We Don't Deserve, Lewis B. Smedes (HarperCollins)

How to Have That Difficult Conversation You've Been Avoiding, Dr. Henry Cloud and Dr. John Townsend (Zondervan)

GRACE, Max Lucado (Zondervan)

When Life's Not Working: 7 Simple Choices for a Better Tomorrow, Bob Merritt (BakerBooks)

Flight Log

My notes on Forgiveness is a Dirty Word

_____

_____

_____

_____

_____

_____

_____

_____

_____

_____

_____

_____

_____

_____

_____

_____

_____

_____

_____

_____

_____

_____

_____

Your Third Move

Crash Course

Tired

And lonely,
So tired
The heart aches.
Meltwater trickles
Down the rocks,
The fingers are numb,
The knees tremble,
It is now,
Now, that you must not give in.

On the path of the others
Are resting places,
Places in the sun
Where they can meet.
But this
Is your path,
And it is now,
Now, that you must not fail.
Weep
If you can,
Weep,
But do not complain.
The way chose you–
And you must be thankful.

Dag Hammarskjöld
Markings

I WALKED INTO A STAFF MEETING. I expressed my opinion. In less than 24 hours I was out of a job I had for almost eight years. The previous year I'd received the highest performance review of anyone on staff! Job loss is a crushing blow. How do you pay the bills? How do you feed your family? My heart was hijacked that day.

My life has crashed. Your life has crashed. Crashes lurk. They pounce when you're not looking. Twists. Turns. Loss. Agony. Redemption. Life is like that, isn't it? Here's the bad news: It's not going to get better. It's always going to be that way. So, what do you do when everything changes and shifts? What do you do when the crushing weight of life flattens you? What do you do when you fly into the face of a raging storm that's determined to rob you of Altitude?

INNER TUMULT

These questions have haunted mankind as far back as history takes us. They stalk us at night. Therefore, it's only appropriate to look at a story from one of the oldest books around. No one really knows who wrote this book and yet it contains a narrative stunning in its scope of human loss, tragedy, and victory. It has gripped hearts and minds for thousands of years. It seems everyone who finds himself or herself under the crushing weight of life's worst circumstances easily identifies with Job. Job is the guy you never want to be. But one day you look in the mirror and he looks back. Job is beat up and knocked flat. His misfortunes pile up! His wife spews her venomous line—

"Curse God and die!" (Job 2:9)

Job's friends hear of his cataclysmic misfortunes. They come around him in tacit support. They sit on the ground with him for seven days and seven nights. No one says a word, because they see how grievous his suffering is. Silence ensues for 158 hours. The sun comes up, the sun goes down. Silence.

Then, Job speaks out of his crash. He gives voice to the inner tumult.

> After this, Job opened his mouth and cursed the day of his birth. He said: "May the day of my birth perish, and the night it was said, 'A boy is born!' That day—may it turn to darkness; may God above not care about it; may no light shine upon it. What I feared has come upon me; what I dreaded has happened to me I have no peace, no quietness; I have no rest, but only turmoil."
> (Job 3:1-4, 25-27)

Loss and defeat. Twist in the morning. Turn in the evening. Panic. Stress. Your life is shifting fast. Your life has changed forever. The crushing weight of every detail crashes upon you. What do you do now? Where do you go now? Job was the greatest man of his time, a man who had it all. He was wealthy beyond imagination. He was intelligent and had the family others defined their families by. He had everything. He was admired in the community. Respected by everyone. And now his life is decimated in an explosion of unpredictable events that defy every modicum of logic. He doesn't know what to do or where to go. Ever felt like that?

It's hard to read his story and it's even harder to stitch together reasons for such devastation. But it's not hard to see God knows right where Job is. God still knows Job's heart. God knows the depth of his pain and suffering. Job laid it all out with gut-wrenching cries. *None of this makes any sense!* Besides not making sense, it hurt so bad he wishes he were never born. "Obliterate the day I was born," he cries. "Blank out the night I was conceived!" I like the way Eugene Peterson paints it:

"Let it be a black hole in space. May God above forget it ever happened. Erase it from the books! May the day of my birth be buried in deep darkness, shrouded by the fog, swallowed by the night."
(Job 3:4-5 The Message)

But he's not done. He explodes:

"May those who are good at cursing curse that day."
(Job 3:8)

Those who are good at cursing? Really? Go get Eddie Murphy, Chris Rock, and Howard Stern. Give them a crack at it as well. Maybe they can come up with even more creative ways to denigrate this miserable wreck of a birthday!

Ever felt like that?

Job is at his most transparent and vulnerable state when he admits he was always afraid something like this would happen. It always lingered in the back of his mind. Have you ever felt that way? When everything is going perfectly in your life, there's a sinister thought lurking in the shadows whispering, *This can't last, you know. Everything is just too good. It's too perfect. You're too blessed. Any time now, something is going to happen.*

> *No way out. Nothing seems fair.*
> *Nothing makes sense.*

Twist in the morning. Turn in the evening. Job's life crushed him. No way out. Nothing seems fair. Nothing makes sense. Higgs boson explains the universe? [1] Nope, doesn't matter. At this point in Job's story, philosophy and theories of life's origin don't matter at all. At this point in Job's life, religion doesn't matter either.

Brennan Manning wrote, *"In times of persecution theoretical Christianity will collapse."* [2] It has to. Theoretical Christianity can't hold the weight of anything. It wafts away in the wind and evaporates. What you need at this point in your life is a God who is with you. You don't need terra cotta banter and doughnuts. You don't need more social media conversations. You need a God who is with you. Period. But before God can be with you, you need to really *know* God. And, as I see it, there are three prerequisites for really *knowing* God: give up the debate, religion and your expectations.

GIVE UP THE DEBATE

People like to debate the existence of God. It happens all the time. Not long ago, the *Wall Street Journal* had an article titled "Man vs. God." In that article two different points of view were represented. The one viewpoint was by an atheist who didn't want to give God the credit for anything. The other opinion was by a theologian/ philosopher, who was making her presentation about religion.

The atheist started out by saying, *"Darwinian evolution is the only process we have that is ultimately capable of generating anything as complicated as creative intelligences."* [3]

And this is where I go crazy because what he's saying is that it takes evolution to create God. It doesn't make any sense and yet people put this stuff out there! They forget that the theory of evolution is just that—a theory. He goes on to postulate that you have to have evolution to even find a creative intelligence in the universe.

He then summarizes his argument by asking, *"Where does that leave God? The kindest thing to say is that it leaves him with nothing to do, and no achievements that might attract our praise, our worship or our fear. Evolution is God's redundancy notice, his pink slip. But we have to go further. A complex creative intelligence with nothing to do is not just redundant. A divine designer is all but ruled out by the consideration that he must be at least as complex as the entities he was wheeled out to explain. God is not dead. He was never alive in the first place."*

On the other side, a woman who writes about religion answers him. She argues:

> "Religion was not supposed to provide explanations that lay within the competence of reason, but to help us live creatively with realities for which there are no easy solutions." [4]

Now that's interesting, because there are a lot of things to which there are no easy solutions. So, is that what religion or God ultimately does—gives us a way to live in a new reality where we can figure everything out by using creative juice?

She continues:

"The best theology is a spiritual exercise akin to poetry. Religion is not an exact science but a kind of art form that, like music or painting, introduces us to a mode of knowledge that is different from the purely rational and which cannot easily be put into words. At its best it holds us in an attitude of wonder."

In that article two very bright people squared off. On one side, there is no God. There can't be a God. Evolution really is the only thing we have and if there is an intelligent designer, he had to evolve out of the evolving evolvement. On the other side, the artisan theologian comes along, pats him on the back, and essentially says:

But religion is a comfort. Religion is like a poem. It's like art and it develops. We can find some meaning, comfort, and purpose in it. And two smart people are ultimately wrong. Two smart people are missing the point. They didn't get it on that particular day because both of their positions were well rooted and grounded in God being transcendent. *If there is a God up there, He would have to be like this. If there is a God up there then religion is kind-of-like this.* They both live at the dead end of opinion.

All of that changes when God is immanent. It all changes when God is right here, right now. It all changes when God lives in you, through you, and with you. That's the God of the Bible. That God is not transcendent. He is not some aloof entity somewhere out there disconnected and detached from the affairs of mankind. The God of the Bible is Emmanuel—God *with* us. The God of the Bible says, *I will come into your world and I will be with you. I will be for you, and I will give My life so you can have life forever with Me.* Immanence astounds us.

PHILOSOPHY 101

How you understand God really matters, especially when your whole life crashes around you. In that reality, you survive only by reaching out to a God who is right here, personal and very, very real. This move is a decision of the heart.

Be that as it may, people continue to love the debate. What about the people who are hungry? What about the people who never get to hear about God? What about all the injustice in the world? What about evolution?

That's what I had to do four decades ago. I had to give up the debate. I took Philosophy 101, thinking I would lasso all the answers to life. I took psychology and political science, thinking these primordial ingredients to society would unlock the mysteries of my life. The result? I ended up a Spanish major, driving a cab to New York airports.

I had to give up the debate when I went to a Midwest university asking theoretical questions about God. My friends there gently swayed me beyond existential questions to the immanence of Him. I began to see there was no other way to go. I was stuck in front of Jesus. I had to make a decision of the heart. You will rarely find God in the debate room. You will, instead, often find Him with people whose lives are crashing down. He finished the debate 2000 years ago. I let Him finish my debate.

GIVE UP RELIGION

Yes, you read that correctly. Religion, by its very nature, says, God's up there and I'm down here. So, if I get enough of my spiritual affairs and my good deeds in order, then I'm building a platform I can stand on at the end of time, and God will see I was really, really good. It's not about that. Not at all. What was Abraham's religion? Didn't have one. Just talked to God. If you get into religion, you just bought yourself a performance treadmill. The other problem, of course, is you're always flying blind. You never really know where you are. *Did I do enough? Did I put enough points on the board?* If it's about performance and being in the right place at the right time, we are all up a creek without the proverbial paddle. It doesn't work that way. You've got to give that up. God's always been relational. Time to drop religion. Time to decide. Time to gain Altitude.

GIVE UP YOUR EXPECTATIONS

If we're really honest, we'll admit we sometimes have expectations that life is somehow going to magically make us feel better and give us a higher sense of personal significance. However, the accumulation of cool stuff and zippy personal experiences will only take us so far. Your Altitude is solidly defined by God's immediacy, not magical expectations.

I was in my favorite chair watching ESPN and the food channel at the same time. These are among the most important things in my life—watching sports and watching people eat. As I was going back and forth between the two, I flashed by the MTV Music Awards and saw they were giving Taylor Swift an award for best music video. This talented young girl was about to deliver the speech of her life. She was overwhelmed. You could see, in her youthful exuberance, she wanted to capture and cherish this moment forever. Suddenly, Kanye West storms the stage. He grabs the microphone and makes it clear to Taylor and the rest of the world he doesn't think Taylor should've won the award. Taylor was visibly shaken and thrown off her game. However, I could see it becoming a great opportunity. In an unscripted crazy moment, she learned quickly that awards and the adoration of millions don't have the power to push back the crash. Crashes lurk and pounce. Altitude is what you do after the crash.

The depth of what you need to know about yourself comes from an immanent God who loves you, cares about you, entered the world to meet you. At some point there's going to be someone who shows up to steal your thunder and ruin your moment. That's your learning moment. That sets up your move toward Altitude.

THE NEED FOR HOPE

Not long ago, Princeton University did a study on the one word that's most often used verbally and in print. They thought the word was going to be *love*. Instead, they found the word was *hope*.

That's what human beings need most of all. We need a lot of love to be sure. Pop music relentlessly reminds us of that. But we need massive amounts of hope. We need to hope there's a God who will come alongside us when our lives are crushed and we don't know who to talk to or where to go. Hope is a prelude to Altitude.

At some point in our lives, we've all been where Job was. Life crushed us. We didn't know where to go. We didn't know what to do. We didn't know who to talk to. Twists and turns. Agony. Maybe you're at one of these places right now. Maybe you've been there before. My prediction is you will crash at one of these places in the future.

A CRASH COURSE

We crash *relationally*. Relationships are unpredictable. The engagement is over. A marriage slides toward oblivion. A co-worker trashes you. A friend misrepresents what you said. Quite often, they don't turn out to be what we think they're supposed to be. A song laments, *How can people be so heartless? How can people be so cruel?* [5] It doesn't make sense. We get caught in the vortex of relational messes and we find ourselves crashing.

We crash *financially*. We see that all around us. We read it in the paper every day. We're in the worst financial mess in a generation. There hasn't been this kind of uncertainty and fear since The Great Depression. *Where's this money thing going? Is the economy ever going to come back? Is my financial life ever going to straighten out?* Our homes, our bank accounts, our pension funds are mired in uncertainty. One false move and it all crashes to the ground.

We crash *professionally*. One minute our career is going in a certain direction and at the drop of a hat it takes a nosedive or spins off into a black hole somewhere. Think about how many people woke up one day and went to work as they normally have for years never suspecting anything would change. Like me, by the end of the day nothing is ever the same again. No job. Hijacked? What's next?

We crash *serially*. In other words, we oftentimes go through a series of crashes. Maybe there is a relational crash that's followed by a financial crash. That leads to a career crash and suddenly it's just crash, crash, crash! You don't know what to do to gain Altitude. You hope and pray there's a way out.

We crash *emotionally*. We don't know how to feel, what we feel, or if we'll ever feel better again. We hope we will rebound.

But numbness sets in and dulls emotional resilience.

We crash *familially*. That means we crash inside of our own families. Families aren't immune from the crashing and struggle. Brother to brother, sister to sister, sister to brother, parent to child. Family life crashes and we don't know if we're going to get out of the pugilistic debacle to live normally again.

We crash *medically*. A routine physical reveals the worst. An x-ray pulls back the curtain on an enemy lurking inside. Multiple medical interventions take you nowhere. A loved one's life hangs between the trapeze of life and death. Medical crashes usher us into the twilight zone of anxiety.

We crash *spiritually*. We get lost along the way. We start out with great expectations following a God we thought was there for us then suddenly we're in darkness. Out of the blue everything we know goes poof! Like Thomas, we're not sure He's there. *Deus absconditus*. Enter dark night of the soul stage left. Elijah went through his spiritual crash in 1 Kings 19. Now it's your turn to cry out in anguish.

DENOUEMENT

The point is, nearly every crash runs on a predictable track. I call it the crash circuit. There are warnings seen or unseen. Did you notice that a year after our economy crashed all the armchair quarterbacks were suddenly pointing out the warnings that nobody saw (but were right in front of our eyes) before the crash? There are warnings seen or unseen. There are sneaky, wobbling dominoes that ultimately fall. There is a moment during the crashing when you know you're undone. You're down and out for the count. Then there's a *denouement (day-noo-mahn)*, a fancy French word for a definitive ending. It's the conclusion, the cessation. The crash happened. The crash ended. It's vitally important to understand there is life beyond the crash. There is always life beyond the crash.

Several things may happen at that point. The first is, you may actually figure out the meaning behind the entire crash, dominoes and all. You may see it all with crystal clarity and say, "Ah! Now I understand what happened!" Keep in mind Job never had that privilege. Despite God restoring his body, his wealth and his family, we're never told Job was allowed to peer behind the heavenly curtain to see the deeper meaning behind his crash. God never gave him an explanation.

Redeeming the crash is also one of the possible outcomes. When we redeem something, we pick up all the broken fragments of the crash and we allow God to use them and rebuild them. It's the former addict who now counsels addicts. It's the grieving father who agrees to donate his daughter's organs, after a car accident, to save three other people. It's the woman whose 15-year-old daughter takes her own life and she breathes life into a suicide prevention program.

But the greatest outcome of a crash is when you listen to God and follow Him more closely than you ever have before. I believe that's the real point of all crashes. To know what He wants from your life. To know what He is able to do in and through your life above and beyond the crash. Don't get stuck in demanding fairness. Fairness is only an excuse to have your way. At the heart of fairness is self-centeredness. Fairness is a dead end. If you demand it, sooner or later you'll hit that wall. Fairness ultimately cheats you out of knowing God deeply. While it's never easy, those who listen to God and learn to follow Him more closely will gain Altitude beyond the crash.

CRASH AND LEARN

The phone call came in the middle of the night from my brother-in-law, Jeff. His wife was coming home late in the evening down a winding country road. I've been on that road. It twists and turns and rattles and rolls. Lisa's car hit gravel and spun off the road into a tree. She died on impact. It's the call you never want to get. We went to Pennsylvania to be with Jeff and his two teenage children who just lost their mom. All we could do in that moment was to be there during the worst crash imaginable.

Many years went by. It was a beautiful evening in a candlelit church on a small country road in Pennsylvania. Jeff was getting married. I was officiating the wedding, standing there looking at his smiling face and the joyous face of his new bride. Candles were lit, words were spoken, and new vows were exchanged. A beautiful moment. But it crashed. There wasn't enough relational glue to hold it together. No Altitude. Short flight.

How easy it would have been for Jeff to throw up his arms in the ultimate *"It's not fair"* to God after two monumental crashes. But today Jeff has a great marriage with a wonderful woman. I love to be with them. Their life is a life of grace and love. You can feel it when you're in their presence. Jeff lives in the redemptive moment. He would be the first to tell you, *"I know God more deeply today than ever before. I know the heart of God more deeply today than over 20 years ago when everything crashed and crushed my soul."*

My life has crashed. Your life has crashed. Crashes lurk. They pounce when you're not looking. Here's the flight plan for resilience. *Let your crash become a crash course in getting to know God better.* Like Job, you may never know the reason for the crash, but rest assured God is shaping, molding, and refining you through it. Despite the agony and broken pieces, He is working all things together so you can gain Altitude.

My crash? It started the best twenty years of my life.

Dear Michael,

I know you so often live in the valley of the shadow of the questions. Why did this happen? Why did my heart have to be broken? Why didn't I see it coming? What do I do now? Will I ever get over or beyond this? In this valley I will walk with you beyond your crash.

Sometimes there will be a holy emptiness where confusion, anger and grief seem to inundate your soul. You will feel like you are choking on anxiety and gasping for sanity. I know those are the most difficult of days for you. I will walk with you through those days and, in our walking, we will come to another valley.

This will be the valley of holy reasons. It doesn't exist on any map. It doesn't exist in your world. You only get there with Me taking you. As you look at them, these reasons may often seem illogical and out of place. Some will seem to hurt and cause conflict. That will be because they were crafted in a place you haven't been to yet. A place where My perfect will knits all things together for good purposes that are always infused with holy reasons.

In the valley of holy reasons I will whisper to you. You won't know when I will whisper, however, so you must always be listening quite carefully. It may be in the night just before you fall asleep, when your weary heart is worn down from being so long in the valley of questions. It may be in the middle of reading a passage of scripture when a holy reason is gently spoken to your soul and you feel your mind overwhelmed by a flash of unexpected peace. Or it may arrive surreptitiously in a dream, allowing entrance to a mysterious balm of holiness that begins to heal jagged grief or relational brokenness. I may even decide the best way to get it to you is through one who has crashed before and is now ready to share his or her holy reason with you.

You must keep walking and wait for the whisper. I will get it to you at the best time which will knit all times together. You will never be the same after your crash (being the same is not the point), but you will always be stronger in an illogical way. Your strength will come from trusting what you cannot see and living for what you can only hope for. There isn't a reason for everything that happens and that makes for difficult days. But a reason finds everything. My holy reason will find you and give you Altitude.

We will move past your crash,

God

Air Traffic Control

1. What was your worst crash ever?

_____

_____

_____

_____

2. What's the best principle you learned from crashing?

_____

_____

_____

_____

3. Which of the Crash Courses can you check off from your experiences in the past?

    ❏ relationally   ❏ financially

    ❏ careerially   ❏ serially

    ❏ emotionally   ❏ familially

    ❏ medically   ❏ spiritually

4. As a group, read 1 Kings 19.

List what happens to Elijah sequentially.

_____

_____

_____

5. Which act speaks into where you are in your spiritual life now?

_____

_____

_____

6. Who do you know who has redeemed a crash? Tell that story.

_____

_____

_____

Flying Higher

Rebuilding your Broken World, Gordon MacDonald (Thomas Nelson)

Nice Girls Don't Change the World, Lynne Hybels
(Willow Creek Association)

Necessary Endings, Dr. Henry Cloud (HarperCollins)

Tough Choices, Carly Fiorina (Penguin Group)

Now What Do I Do?: The Surprising Solution When Things Go Wrong,
Dr. John Townsend (Zondervan)

Flight Log

My notes on Crash Course

_____

_____

_____

_____

_____

_____

_____

_____

_____

_____

_____

_____

_____

_____

_____

_____

_____

_____

_____

_____

_____

_____

_____

_____

_____

Your Fourth Move

Shift the Sexual Vortex

O my luve's

like a red, red rose
That's newly sprung in June;
O my luve's like the melodie
That's sweetly played in tune.

As fair art thou, my bonnie lass,
So deep in luve am I;
And I will luve thee still, my dear,
Till a' the seas gang dry.

Till a' the seas gang dry, my dear,
And the rocks melt wi' the sun:
O I will luve thee still, my dear,
When the sands o' life shall run.

And fare thee weel, my only luve,
And fare thee weel a while!
And I will come again, my luve,
Though it were ten thousand mile.

Robert Burns
A Red, Red Rose

WE'VE COME A LONG WAY from the red, red rose. Cellina dreamed of an extraordinary, artistic future. She wanted to be a singer, play in an orchestra, go to school, and get her degree. Years of dreaming and visualizing her passion finally paid off as she was accepted into a prestigious music school. This should have been a time of rejoicing and celebrating for Cellina, but very quickly reality set in. "I had just taken out too many student loans," she realized. "I couldn't take out any more."

The price of Cellina's dream came to a staggering $10,000 per semester. She worked three jobs and realized her jobs left very little time for school, which defeated the creation of her future. What she did next was either ingenious or shocking, depending on whom you ask. Cellina went online and found a website that offered to connect "sugar daddies" with "sugar babies"—essentially men who were willing to support younger women financially in exchange for their companionship. Make no mistake about it, *companionship* is not the bottom line—and the women know it. It's all justified under the rationale that this is simply two adults engaged in a financial arrangement where both parties are getting their needs met. The sad reality of Cellina's situation is that many are following in her footsteps. The idea that sex is so much more than a benign three-letter word has somehow escaped the conscience of our culture.

DESIGNED FOR CONNECTION

We are overwhelmed by sex. We are overrun by sex. We are hijacked by overt sensuality. At the same time, we are underwhelmed by truth. The next new gadget fascinates and preoccupies us while we are overly cautious about God. That's the spinning, churning culture we live in today. It's nothing short of a tragedy waiting to happen in your relational life. It's what I call the sexual vortex. A vortex is a spinning, violent, spiral motion. Tornadoes and hurricanes are examples of a vortex. The thing about a vortex is that once it begins, it picks up steam fast. It tears up everything in its path. When we see 6 o'clock news stories of devastation they're always hard to believe.

Make no mistake about it; we were designed by God to desire passionate love. We yearn for goose bump connection. We are starved for relational engagement. We want to fully understand what it means to have a mind, a soul, and a body. So we write lyrics and sing songs about pounding hearts and visceral connecting. Songs of vivid connection have been written throughout generations.

> My lover is radiant and ruddy,
>> outstanding among ten thousand.
> His head is purest gold;
>> his hair is wavy
>> and black as a raven.
> How beautiful your sandaled feet,
>> O prince's daughter!
> Your graceful legs are like jewels,
>> the work of a craftsman's hands.
> (Song of Songs 5:10-11, 7:1)

There's amazing passion in those words. The feeling is about bodies and souls. Man and woman were built for joyous connection. But when the melding of hearts isn't understood in the context of God's thought process, and when the great driving need for connection is marred by a culture that sexualizes everything, we end up in a sexual vortex that cuts a path of destruction through our bodies and souls. Whether it's the TV sitcom flirting with sexual tension, Lady Gaga's in-your-face lyrical shockers, the latest movers and shakers' sex scandal, or Dr. Drew interviewing a pastor and his wife about biblical sexuality in prime time, we are surrounded by a sexualized society.

THE ROAD TO TIMNAH

Mark Driscoll, pastor of Mars Hill Church in Seattle, Washington, has written a book with his wife, Grace, called *Real Marriage: The Truth about Sex, Friendship, and Life Together*. They write:

"The worship of sex as a god is as passionate as ever. The sexual revolution of the 1960s and '70s radically altered the sexual landscape of our nation so that today, sex before marriage and viewing pornography are the culturally accepted norm. Subsequently, we are in the midst of a sexual social experiment the consequence of which no one truly knows.

Only by seeing sex as a god we worship are we able to make sense of the porno plague. The statistics paint an ugly picture. Annual pornography revenues are more than $90 billion worldwide. In the United States, pornography revenues were $13 billion in 2006, more than all combined revenues of professional football, baseball, and basketball franchises or the combined revenues of ABC, CBS, and NBC ($6.2 billion). Porn sites account for 12% of all Internet sites. Everyday 2.5 pornographic e-mails are sent.

A staggering 90% of children between the ages of eight and sixteen have viewed pornography on the Internet, in most cases unintentionally. The average age of first Internet exposure to pornography is eleven." [1]

It's a tragedy. The sexual vortex brings hurt, pain, and tragedy all the time. The Bible doesn't shy away from the truth about sex, friendships, and life together. Let's look at a story you might be familiar with.

> Samson went down to Timnah and saw there a young Philistine woman. When he returned, he said to his father and mother, "I have seen a Philistine woman in Timnah; now get her for me as my wife."
> (Judges 14:1-2)

Hook me up, Mommy. Hook me up, Daddy. I saw this girl and I am ready to rock 'n' roll. *Get her for me.*

The next part of the story relates his courtship, the negotiations between families, and the protracted wedding celebration. He's got 30 guys involved. This can't be a good idea. Then there's a wager and a riddle. That's not sounding good, either.

> On the fourth day, they said to Samson's wife, "Coax your husband into explaining the riddle for us, or we will burn you and your father's household to death. Did you invite us here to rob us?"
> Then Samson's wife threw herself on him, sobbing, "You hate me! You don't really love me. You've given my people a riddle, but you haven't told me the answer."

"I haven't even explained it to my father or mother," he replied, "so why should I explain it to you?" She cried the whole seven days of the feast. So on the seventh day he finally told her, because she continued to press him. She in turn explained the riddle to her people.

Before sunset on the seventh day the men of the town said to him,

"What is sweeter than honey?
What is stronger than a lion?"

Samson said to them,

"If you had not plowed with my heifer,
you would not have solved my riddle."

Then the Spirit of the Lord came upon him in power. He went down to Ashkelon, struck down thirty of their men, stripped them of their belongings and gave their clothes to those who had explained the riddle. Burning with anger, he went up to his father's house. And Samson's wife was given to the friend who had attended him at his wedding.

(Judges 14:15-20)

Plowed with my heifer? What's that about? The Bible doesn't shy away from the truth about sex, friendship, dating, and all those things related to who we are in relational tension. The story is as well written as an Emmy-winning mini-series.

By the time you get to Judges 16, you can see the end of the road.

One day Samson went to Gaza, where he saw a prostitute. He went in to spend the night with her. The people of Gaza were told, "Samson is here!" So they surrounded the place and lay in wait for him all night at the city gate. They made no move during the night, saying, "At dawn we'll kill him." (Judges 16:1-2)

The pitiable dead end of Samson comes as no surprise.

Then his brothers and his father's whole family went down to get him. They brought him back and buried him between Zorah and Eshtaol in the tomb of Manoah his father. He had led Israel twenty years.
(Judges 16:31)

Samson could have gone down in history as perhaps one of the greatest leaders ever. We could be remembering Samson today for his wisdom, political savvy, and constructive strength. Instead, we remember him as being destroyed by the sexual vortex and the lies that the vortex slings our way.

VISUAL JUGGERNAUT

Maybe you've heard some of these lies about sex:

There is nothing more fulfilling than sex
It doesn't matter what you do with your body
You can't get hurt in a consenting sexual relationship
You need to have experience, so you might as well start in high school
Having sex before marriage or outside of your marriage is no big deal
It doesn't matter what you allow yourself to look at

or fantasize about.

It doesn't matter what you do when you're single again at 58

People end up believing a lot of these lies. Our society's structures are oftentimes based on a lot of these lies. When we build a culture on lies the culture will crumble under a weight of deception. Nothing built on lies can last.

Recently, my wife and I got away for our break after Christmas. We went to see our daughter in New York. Ashley, who is an architect, invited us to breakfast the next day. Afterward, I was to take a tour of her company's new building project. They were restoring an old New York landmark. We made our way down to Soho, a very eclectic area in lower Manhattan. We walked down Wooster Street to the front of this stately building built in 1890. Ashley led me inside and showed me the first floor with its beautiful white columns. You could see the restoration process in a stark reality of dirt and debris. It was fascinating. But the real action was below street level.

Workers were lowering the floor of the basement—digging it out, to create usable office space. The most interesting architectural feature to me were the beams holding up the building, for more than 120 years. I got up as close as I could to these rugged beams. They were rough-hewn. Their strength was awe inspiring. I couldn't help but think about the engineers, more than 120 years ago, who got together and said, *"We need something that'll hold this building up forever."* They created the future. These old wooden behemoths are as good today as they were over a century ago.

This visual juggernaut speaks to the truth about our fragile lives. Unless we are being supported by something to hold the weight of all the years, the sexual vortex is more than capable of tearing it all down in an instant. So, what are your beams? What holds up your life?

MASS DELUSION

In a *Vanity Fair* article on our current economic crisis, writer Joseph Stiglitz made the following brilliant statement:

> "Even when we fully repair the banking system, we'll still be in deep trouble... because we were already in deep trouble. In the years leading up to the recession the bottom 80 percent of the American population had been spending around 110 percent of its income. What made this level of indebtedness possible was the housing bubble. As we now know, this enabled banks to lend and households to borrow on the basis of assets whose value was determined in part by mass delusion." [2]

What's most interesting are the two words *mass delusion*. In other words, everybody was doing crazy stuff that would result in chaos and would ultimately bring everything down, but they kept moving *toward* the chaos. They kept moving into the financial vortex.

We're in the same mass delusion today in regard to our sexuality. We can see it vortexing in light of the fiscal reality we've entered into. But the grand irony is that no matter how clearly we see it operating all around us, we are still blind to the sexual vortex. It's the ever present desecrated byproduct of an immeasurably rich gift God gave long ago.

THE HIDDEN SECRET

Let's clear up a ubiquitous misconception. There is a huge difference between "body sex" and the person-centered sexuality God created. Body sex is free from emotional involvement or attachment and is basically exploitative. Therefore, sexuality becomes merely a packaged commodity that can be relationally traded without demands. That's what Cellina is doing during her college years. She's trading sexuality as a commodity. *I'll give you this, you give me that. It's a win-win situation. Right?* It may look that way to her, but it's not going to hold up the rest of her life. She's eroding the foundation of integrity undergirding her life. She's cutting into the beams. Spirituality is not just relevant but also essential to working out an authentic sexuality.

In his book, *The Erotic Word: Sexuality, Spirituality and the Bible*, David Carr states:

> "...sexuality and spirituality are intricately interwoven...when one is impoverished, the other is warped...there is some kind of crucially important connection between the journey toward God and the journey toward coming to terms with our own sexual embodiment." [3]

Too often, cultures that become weak in understanding the support necessary for relationships to work engage in a vortex of unsatiated sexual obsession and sex as a negotiable body experience. And that's where we are. Read the paper. Look at the magazines. Watch TV. Go to the movies. Un-satiated sexual obsession and sex as a negotiable body experience rule the day. The sexual vortex is the unrelenting pursuit of body sex without ever apprehending true sexual fulfillment, and there are two main tensions driving it.

1. Lack of commitment to biblical truth.
2. Lack of discipline of emotional/physical urges.

In reality the sexual vortex can only deliver relational brokenness and emptiness, leaving confusion and emotional pain in its wake. People fall into it all the time. Why? Because the vortex preys on the one scandalous thing that is so easily misunderstood and squandered by men and women—the fact that God *designed* the original sexual vortex. He designed it for good and to be experienced in the proper context of sexual expression.

When you return to Genesis 1 and 2, you'll find that those are the only two chapters in the Bible showing us what God's intent for humanity was before sin entered the equation. You catch a glimpse of the beauty and wonder. You see the incomprehensible picture of how everything was designed to work together. In that picture you see a man and a woman who are created to be together; they are created to be equal partners. They are created to experience life deeply.

> *God created the original sexual vortex.*

But that's all predicated on the basis of one incredibly poignant principle. Man and woman's connectedness is dependent on a vital relationship with God. There was intimacy with God, therefore there was intimacy with the man and the woman. And everything was good. But it all falls apart because of temptation, lack of discipline, and because of the squirrelly ways our minds work. God created the original sexual vortex. He designed it to be experienced in a unique committed relationship. Spirituality and sexuality were designed to be swirling together. *The fact is coming together as male and female in marriage is a living picture of who God is.* When it becomes anything less, it misses the original vortex of the Creator.

We live in a culture invested in keeping this a secret. If this concept, of a swirling spiritual sexual vortex, was so important in our culture, it would be seen everywhere. You'd see it on billboards, in advertisements, and on prime time TV commercials. You'd hear it in political speeches. Instead, we live in a culture with a vested interest in keeping the original vortex a secret. Therefore, we tacitly allow the destruction of our culture from a psychological sexual perspective when we don't push back. We need to shift the sexual vortex to its original design.

> *The fact is coming together as male and female in marriage is a living picture of who God is.*

VORTEX PRINCIPLES

Sex is *right* for so many reasons. But it's also wrong for many other reasons. Here are six of them.

1) When sex is used as a substitute for emotional growth in facing maturity
2) When I'm just unable to say no
3) When sex is used to control and manipulate

4) When sex is used for body pleasure alone

5) When sex is used to gain status in a social system

6) When sex is a commodity traded for mutually exclusive benefits

The sexual vortex can be vicious. It can bring you into self-delusion, as it did to Cellina. Paul puts it this way.

> Flee from sexual immorality. All other sins a man commits are outside his body, but he who sins sexually sins against his own body. Do you not know that your body is a temple of the Holy Spirit, who is in you, whom you have received from God? You are not your own; you were bought at a price. Therefore honor God with your body. (1 Corinthians 6:18-20)

BACK TO THOSE BEAMS

These vortex principles will be the structural beams for your future.

You have free will

You choose everything you do. God's greatest gift, when misused, can sometimes be our biggest curse. With free will comes an amazing obligation to choose the right things. Choose what will edify not what will destroy. Everything is permissible for me but not everything is beneficial.

Not all choices will yield good results

Discernment is always necessary. Again, everything is permissible for me but I will not be mastered by anything. You have to take a look down the road. What comes out of this next decision? Not all choices will yield good results. Discernment is crucial.

God wants your body

Spirituality precedes sexuality. The body is not meant for sexual immorality but for manifesting spiritual maturity and the joy that emanates from the integration of spirit and sex.

Your actions reflect your values and commitments

Everything you do paints a picture of who you really are at the deepest place in your life. What you do reveals an *inside* story.

Discipline means setting limits on temptation

Flee. Set limits. Get out of there. Move away. The best time to make those decisions about discipline is before you have to flee so you know when to flee and why you have to flee. And you understand what it's all about as you put the picture together.

The Spirit will help you maintain discipline

God is invested in you. He's invested in you becoming everything good that you are supposed to be. Maintaining physical discipline is always a good move.

Honor God with your body

Make this a priority. Don't fall into the mass delusion of the cultural sexual vortex. Don't believe the lies that are there to destroy you. Don't be wooed by a society that says body sex is all there is and it's the highest value you can subscribe to.

Shift the Sexual Vortex. Your Altitude depends on it.

Dear Michael,

Today I have to start out with some don'ts. Don't believe the lies about sex. Don't get caught in the sexual vortex. Don't just have body sex and miss the whole point. Don't lose sight of the fact that I created sex in the beginning along with everything else in the universe.

Let me tell you about what I created. Sex tells a story. Sex sings a song. Sex makes a connection. Sex paints commitment in the space between two people. Sex speaks into the future. Sex was designed for unconditional love. Sex was intended for marriage. Sex is a symbol of My unity. Sex gives you an experience of sweeping joy that emanates from a deep place in My heart. Sex is good when you choose for it to be good.

When sex becomes a god, problems abound and you are ambushed by unruly desires. Those desires deface and defame what I most wanted for you in the beginning. I wanted you to experience what I experience. Intimacy. So honor Me with your body. Honor the life I gave you as a gift. Honor the community of faith. Children need examples of men and women who struggle yet live with integrity amidst a culture voracious in its appetite to lure you into disingenuous patterns of behavior.

Set limits on temptation. Reach for intimacy.

I gave My life for you because you were exquisitely

crafted in redemptive holiness. I gave My life for you because grace was worth dying for. Bring spirit and sex together, and you will understand how truth sets you free from emotional or physical entanglements that seek to snare your soul.

I'm here to help you where you're hurting.

Don't believe the lies. Believe Me.

Time for beams. Shift the vortex. Your Move.

God

Air Traffic Control

1. Where do you struggle with being surrounded by a sexualized culture driven by titillation and superficial freedoms?

_____

_____

_____

_____

_____

2. What are the lies about sex you see prevalent around you? Where you work? In your family? In your church or neighborhood?

_____

_____

_____

_____

_____

3. Which sexual vortex principle(s) do you need to reaffirm?

_____

_____

_____

_____

_____

4. What speaks to you from the poem by Robert Burns?

_____

_____

_____

_____

5. Define *connection* as you knew it in your family at age 12.

_____

_____

_____

_____

6. Define it for yourself today.

_____

_____

_____

_____

Flying Higher

Love at Last Sight, Kerry and Chris Shook (Waterbrook Multnomah)

Love, Sex, and Lasting Relationships, Chip Ingram (Baker Books)

Sex God: Exploring the Endless Connections Between Sexuality and Spirituality, Rob Bell (HarperOne)

Beyond Sex Roles, Gilbert Bilezikian (Baker Acedemic)

Flight Log

My notes on Shift the Sexual Vortex

Your Fifth Move

Seize Courage

Too often

*I hesitate to take courageous action because I don't
want to put decades of work on the line. Sometimes I
say to myself, "I've taken enough hits. I don't want to
take any more risks. I don't want to expend myself to
the limits one more time." But when I feel this way,
I try to remember Esther, who said, 'I'll do the right
thing...and if I perish, I perish.'
I need Esther's courage.
Lots of us leaders do.*

Bill Hybels
Courageous Leadership

ESTHER. Luther wanted to dump her in the 16th century. The great medieval Jewish theologian and physician, Maimonides, rated it as one of the greatest holy books ever written. Surprisingly, there's no mention of God. Yet He stealthily weaves His way through each dramatic scene. Esther makes two moves with trembling faith—

> You must let go of your will to trust God's plan.
> You must act decisively at the moment God's plan
> cuts through the core of your life.

There are multiple ways to teach truth. One way is to use drama. Yet another is to focus on ancient cultural meanings and word definitions. Another way is to tell a story letting *veritas* speak to the listener's heart. Esther was always meant to be a story. Let me tell it to you.

DICE DAYS

Once upon a time, there was a king, who was a little bit greedy. OK, he was a *lot* greedy. There was another man named Haman who had too much ambition mixed with anger, and there was a wise uncle with a very beautiful niece. These four lived in an ancient city that was the capital of one of the most powerful countries in the old world.

Everything was going so well for the king that he decided to host a big party for his best friends. When he gave a party it was of the marathon variety. This party lasted six months! As the end of the party approached, the king thought a little icing on the cake would be nice, so he opened up the festival to everyone in the city for seven fun-filled days of wine, food, and music. The king, who was a little tipsy at the time, decided he wanted an indelible grand finale for the festivities. What better ultimate event than to show off his beautiful wife, Vashti. But he decided this before asking her, which is something you should never do if you're married—even if you are the king!

The king wanted the queen to put herself on display before all the men of the city. Just stand there in all her dazzling glory and let everybody take a good, long look. Well, the queen did not think this was a particularly good idea and she told the king to forget it. The Bible doesn't tell us what else she said, which was probably plenty. So, the king goes for counseling because he is really mad. He wants to get some accurate feedback, which in "*Kingspeak,*" means he wants one of the wise men to tell him *he's right and she's wrong*. This is pretty much what men think counseling is. These wise consultants, realizing where room and board come from, held a brief conference. They quickly realized they had a bigger problem than meets the royal eye. The queen's refusal to acquiesce to the king's wishes and publicly humiliate him was not simply a normal incident of marital mayhem, but an act of high treason against the kingdom! All the men nodded to acknowledge their high level of anxiety.

"If we let this fly," they reasoned, "all women will feel they can do whatever they want, whenever they want. Next thing you know, they'll take our jobs and we'll be watching the babies while they go out on business lunches. The whole cushy system as we know it will grind to a halt! But if we act swiftly, we may be able to delay the Women's Movement for at least a couple of thousand years. By then, who cares? It's not our problem anymore."

The good ol' boys chortled and patted themselves on the back like men do when they think they've gotten out of a tight jam. Here was the prescription to getting rid of this particular headache: Get the king to divorce the queen and get someone who's easier to manipulate. Someone beautiful, but passive. Someone who likes to sit around and count her blessings all day. Someone who's more content watching *Rachel Ray* make date pudding than *The Real Housewives of Persia*. Momentum was moving in their favor. Momentum is good. The king was pleased.

As planned, he divorced Vashti. Then he circulated a proclamation that all husbands were to be kings in their own homes (a law which many husbands invoke to this day) and that wives should be happy just to be in the palace! But there was one final decree of decrees. A national beauty contest was to be organized to select a new queen! Think *The Bachelor* with a cast of thousands.

This seemed to make all the men happy. It created a new economic boom. The market was flooded with lots of new jobs like regional coordinators for the beauty contest, beauty school franchises and a new line of makeup from Egypt, which providentially became the world's first Pyramid marketing business. Hopeful maidens flooded the city, coming from places far and wide. They arrived by the caravan load, some on parade-style floats, others in wagons with chickens and Grandma in the back. After 12 months of mandatory beauty treatments (designed to take care of skin roughed by wind and sand) and toning up with Cleopatra's Zumba workout system, the king started to meet the candidates one by one for the preliminary elimination rounds.

Time passed. The king was in no big rush to make a hasty decision and, not wanting to disturb interest rates which had fallen to an all time low, he kept the program going for about four years. After more than 1,000 queen-wannabes were interviewed, the king met his match. A young stunner named Esther became the ruby in his crown and she was named queen at a hastily called press conference. The king was ecstatic about his decision and it prompted an altruistic floodgate to burst forth. He announced aggressive tax rebates on new camels, Persian rugs, and just about everything else in the kingdom.

This is the part in most epics that ends with the words, *and they all lived happily ever after.* But not this story.

You see, every great story has a villain and this one's no different. A guy named Haman steps into the picture. The story gets a little complicated here, but no more complicated than *LOST*, so if you tracked with Ben, Jack, Kate, and Hurley you'll have no trouble following what ensues.

HER BRAIN WAS ON FIRE WITH GOD

The new queen, Esther, had a cousin, Mordecai, who had a *deep as a well* love for God. Years before, when she became an orphan, he adopted her and took care of her as if he were her father. Mordecai was a good man. While others would bow to Haman, who had been named the king's right-hand man, he would not bow. The power of that vaulted position had quickly gone to Haman's turban. Mordecai's refusal to pay homage made Haman so mad that he went and threw some dice, which is what you did when you were mad in those days. He kept throwing the dice until he got his number and then went to the king with an insidious, misleading request.

"Do you think it would be OK if we killed off a bunch of people who don't keep your laws? They really are a bad example to the rest of the loyal subjects. They have strange ways. And by the way, I can probably handle the details by myself without any trouble to you, your Excellency." The king thought this was a good idea, and he gave Haman his ring, which was like giving him *carte blanche* to the kingdom. Haman then sent a letter to the entire region stating that all the "Chosen" would be erased from the kingdom on the 13th day of the 12th month. The people of the kingdom were perplexed because they knew the "Chosen" were fine people. It all sounded so crazy.

When Esther's cousin, Mordecai, heard about the letter he went into great despair. He even put on special despair clothes and walked around looking funny and attracting a lot of attention. Esther heard about it through the grapevine and sent a message to her uncle asking what the deal was with the despair outfit. She even tried sending him some Brioni suits and Prada shoes. He wasn't having any of it. Instead, he sent word back to his niece of what was happening. He attached a copy of the king's decree and asked her to use some of her queenly capital and speak to the king about this great injustice. Esther was horrified. She sent a message back to Mordecai informing him that no one could go in to see the king unless they were specifically called for, and she hadn't been called for 30 days. Violating this rule could cost someone his or her life. Mordecai sent a note back to her which read, "If you keep silent at this time, God will have to use someone else. But who knows if you have come to the kingdom for such a time as this?"

That's when it happened. There comes a time in your life when you have to grow up. It sneaks up on you sometimes and it stares you in the face. It snuck up on Esther just then. The very words she just read from her cousin both excited her and petrified her. Her brain was on fire with God. She knew what she must do. "If I die, I die." That's just the way it would have to be.

> *Her brain was on fire with God.*

SEIZING COURAGE

Esther was young and beautiful. Hers was the kind of beauty that takes the breath away from young men and causes old men to reminisce of youthful vigor.

Beauty aside, Esther's fairy tale dreams were morphing into an unimaginable nightmare. When she was a girl, she fantasized of becoming a princess. In a fairy tale world fueled by a vibrant, flourishing imagination, she would clap her hands and envision servants bringing sumptuous meals, fine clothes, and colorful banners. Thousands would bow and pay respect to her. Her royal subjects would gladly give their lives for her. What a contrast from this cruel adult world of power struggles, backstabbing and hatred. On this day, she wore a millstone of responsibility around her neck instead of the shining diamonds of her dreams. Whether her people lived or died horribly in a senseless act of genocide was within her power. Was she willing to risk her own life in the transaction? She was too young to be snared in the sticky web of political expediency. Was her beauty a cruel curse? Her selection by Xerxes to be queen hammered the bars of her prison built by rich jesters.

As she meditated on Mordecai's words, she fasted for three days. As the final day of her fast wore on, she felt a deep vacuous ache in her stomach. Her head throbbed. For a moment she thought she would be sick. This plan hatched by her cousin was insane.

Why did I have to say, 'If I die, I die,' she thought.

Then another thought rolled into view.

Abraham, Moses and Joseph were all crazy in their own way. Joshua was kind of quirky. Noah certainly wasn't voted Entrepreneur of the Year before it started raining, either. Somehow God brought all of them through their trials.

Taking a deep breath, she noticed the ache had dissipated. She dressed and walked toward the chamber of her husband, the king. Her beauty was never more radiant. Too many lives cried out from the king's decree of death. She could not ignore this choir of the oppressed. Standing motionless for several minutes she watched the man who ruled an empire as he stared off toward an unlit torch. It appeared he was trying to intimidate it to flame by royal fiat. The torch remained cold. He turned and saw her. Their eyes locked. It was her time, her moment. She knew she had come to the kingdom for this.

THE RIDDLE

"What is it, my sweet?" the king playfully asked. It was difficult for anyone in his position not to be taken aback by her luminous beauty and calming countenance. "What is your request? Even up to half the kingdom, it will be given you."

Esther breathlessly told the king she wanted to throw a splendid dinner party for him and his right-hand man, Haman.

The king was all too happy to oblige because he liked to dine and he liked Haman. So, they had the incomparable meal. Afterward, the king, knowing that his queen's request had to be more substantial than a fancy dinner, queried, "Now, what *is* it you want?" Esther wanted to set everything up just right and decided to make it more like an ancient riddle so she replied to the king, "Tomorrow let us have a second impeccable dinner with just you and Haman. Then I'll tell you!"

Haman's head was swelled three times its normal size over all of the royal attention. He had a private audience to eat with the king and queen not once, but twice! On his way home, he was walking above the dust and smiling even wider as each passing pedestrian bowed in his presence... until he walked by Mordecai again. Mordecai didn't bow down or give him the courtesy of even a look! Haman's mind *raced and raged.*

When he arrived home, he bragged about his audience with the royals but then told his family how despite it all he couldn't enjoy any of it because of Mordecai's stubborn refusal to worship him. His wife, who was sort of a closet terrorist, made a suggestion.

"Why don't you commission a gallows while you're in the king's presence tomorrow and ask his majesty for Mordecai's neck on a rope?"

Haman's eyes got wide. Yes! That would do it! So he commissioned a gallows. Seventy-five feet of impending doom. He wanted a dramatic fall before the rope snapped Mordecai's neck. It had to be high enough so everyone could see. That night Haman slept like a baby.

But God has his own way of dealing with megalomania.

That very night, while Haman gently snoozed, the king

couldn't sleep. He needed some lullaby reading material. Pacing, he finally called for the *Book of Memorable Deeds of the Realm* and had them read aloud.

As it turned out, way before our current story began, Mordecai had heard about an assassination plot on the king. He reported it to the proper authorities and the plot was thwarted. In all the ruckus, the king had never rewarded Mordecai or recognized him for his heroism, but a record of what happened had been dutifully recorded in the *Book of Memorable Deeds of the Realm.*

As the moon reigned above, the king learned for the first time that a courageous citizen hadn't been rewarded for saving his life. He decided then and there to honor Mordecai. However, he would first consult his trusted sidekick, Haman, on the matter.

THE WRONG PARADE

As the sun came up on that fateful day, old Haman was doing a little *I'm On Top of the World* shuffle into the king's court. He was just about ready to ask the king for the neck of Mordecai on the end of a very long rope when the king interrupted.

"Say Haman, we have to honor someone special to me, how shall we do that?"

The king's smile was beguiling.

Haman's ego was about to burst. Knowing for sure that he must be the special one, he quipped, "Let's have a horse and a parade!"

"Great!" exclaimed the king. "Now go and get Mordecai, put him on my horse, with my cloak and crown, and *you, my friend,* will lead the parade!"

Haman felt every nerve ending in his body go numb. He

knew his life was unraveling. As if the humiliation wasn't bad enough, Haman had to lead the prancing horse around the city streets while loudly reading an ironic script: "This is what is done for the man the king delights to honor!"

After the parade, Haman went to dinner with the king and Esther. The king could stand it no longer. He begged Esther to tell him what she wanted. He almost choked when Esther said she just wanted her life and the lives of her people spared because an enemy had planned to wipe them out of existence. Haman's heart sank. The fat lady sang. It was over.

When the king found out it was all Haman's doing, he walked out of the room to gather his thoughts. Haman started begging Esther to have mercy on him. This was a further nail in his coffin because the king returned and thought Haman was assaulting his queen! It was becoming a very bad day for Haman. And it got worse. Haman was hanged on the gallows he had built for Mordecai. It was *his* life that ended in a 75-foot drop.

DICE DAYS FOREVER

Remember how we established that every great story has a villain? Every great story also has a rescuer—sometimes two. Mordecai and Esther were a well oiled machine. They embodied *doing whatever it takes to create their future.* Queen Esther decreed that each year the goodness of God would be remembered at a special time for two days. She called these days *Dice Days.* [1] You see, Haman had thrown the dice against them, but it was his number that came up. Seizing courage is always a good move and makes a good ending to every story of Altitude.

Dear Michael:

I wish I could guarantee everyone would live happily ever after. I can't do that. I can't do that because so much depends on courage. Why did I do it that way? Here it is. Courage emanates from love. This, then, is how life works. I will guarantee My love. Courage will flow from My heart to yours. It will get you home at the end of life's journey. It will lift you up when you go down hard. Courage will be the glue for all the broken pieces of life. And when you think it's finally run its course, I will cause it to quiver within your breast. Your dry heart will soak up the mystery one more time. I made you to love courageously. I made you to beat back the darkness. But you can only accomplish this with Me in you. Remember, a cross etched the way of courage...and I saw that cross the very first moment I dreamed of you. The cross bade Me come to you. The cross is love's dangerous mystery.

Courage is dangerous, Michael, because it puts you in such a vulnerable position. When you have courage you are wide open to be dissected, decimated, and defeated. But in that dangerous position you discover the secret of love's mystery. When you give up, you grow up. When you grant favor to others, you gain favor in return. When you're out of breath from going the distance, the distance becomes the foundation upon which I build your next move. It's that way because only the ones who really want Me run long enough to get Me...and My Kingdom is for those who have panted after the mystery. Dangerous courage is all there is. Live the danger, Michael. Live the lost-ness of the found-ness, live the agony of the celebration, rail against injustice, and drink your fill of amazing grace and know that every time you choose courage you set a light on a hill, urging others to keep running to Me.

Have you ever been in love, Michael? I have. It is good. Remember, courage emanates from love. Altitude waits for you to seize courage, when your brain is on fire with Me.

God

Air Traffic Control

1. Name a courageous person in history.

_____

2. Why did you choose him/her?

_____

_____

_____

_____

_____

3. In what arena of your life do you need to seize courage?

_____

_____

_____

_____

_____

4. Who made a courageous move that impressed you recently?

_____

_____

_____

_____

5. Mordecai and Esther were a team. Are you on a board or team at work where a courageous decision is begging to be made? How can you help catalyze that decision?

_____

_____

_____

_____

6. The letter from God states "courage emanates from love." Do you agree or disagree?

_____

_____

7. As a group read 1 Corinthians 13. Where do you see courage? What words, descriptive of love, are most compelling to you and why?

4 Love is patient, love is kind. It does not envy, it does not boast, it is not proud. 5 It is not rude, it is not self-seeking, it is not easily angered, it keeps no record of wrongs. 6 Love does not delight in evil but rejoices with the truth. 7 It always protects, always trusts, always hopes, always perseveres.
1 Corinthians 13: 4-7 NIV 1984

Love never gives up.
Love cares more for others than for self.
Love doesn't want what it doesn't have.
Love doesn't strut,

Doesn't have a swelled head,

Doesn't force itself on others,

Isn't always "me first,"

Doesn't fly off the handle,

Doesn't keep score of the sins of others,

Doesn't revel when others grovel,

Takes pleasure in the flowering of truth,

Puts up with anything,

Trusts God always,

Always looks for the best,

Never looks back.

But keeps going to the end.

1 Corinthians 13 The Message

Flying Higher

Courageous Leadership, Bill Hybels (Zondervan)

Axiom: Powerful Leadership Proverbs, Bill Hybels (Zondervan)

The Power of a Whisper: Hearing God, Having the Guts to Respond, Bill Hybels (Zondervan)

Winning, Jack Welch with Suzy Welch (HarperCollins)

The Advantage: Why Organizational Health Trumps Everything Else in Business, Patrick Lencioni (Jossey-Bass))

Flight Log

My notes on Seize Courage

_____

_____

_____

_____

_____

_____

_____

_____

_____

_____

_____

_____

_____

_____

_____

_____

_____

_____

_____

_____

_____

_____

_____

_____

Your Sixth Move

Gutsy Conversation

The bird

let loose in eastern skies,
When hastening fondly home,
Ne'er stoops to earth her wing, nor flies
Where idle warblers roam;
But high she shoots through air and light,
Above all low delay,
Where nothing earthly bounds her flight,
Nor shadow dims her way.

So grant me, God, from every care
And stain of passion free,
Aloft, through Virtue's purer air,
To hold my course to Thee!
No sin to cloud, no lure to stay
My Soul, as home she springs;
Thy Sunshine on her joyful way,
Thy Freedom in her wings!

Thomas Moore
The Bird Let Loose

WHEN A DOCTORAL STUDENT at Princeton asked what subjects are left in the world for original dissertation research, Albert Einstein quickly replied, *"Find out about prayer."* [1] He might as well have said take a look at air. You can't see it, can't live without it and much of the time, it works best under pressure.

I RECENTLY HEARD Condoleezza Rice say, "I've always allowed for guidance through ambiguity." [2]

Have you pondered the ambiguities of prayer? Is God listening to everything? What really happens when we pray? If God knows the heart, do you even need words? What if you pray for something you shouldn't pray for? Is there some kind of heavenly prayer-check filter that snuffs out wacky prayer before it hits the ceiling? What if you forget to pray for someone you said you'd pray for? What if you pray for a sports team to win? Is it okay to pray not to suffer? Remember the scene in *Bruce Almighty* when Morgan Freeman steps out of his coveralls and announces he's God? Maybe God is more like that than we think and prayer is just talking to him in a coffee shop way.

Let me tell you a story about a gutsy guy who stood toe to toe with God.

Abraham had a *walk-down-the-road* relationship with God. Religion? Didn't have one. He didn't pack anything cumbersome or complex. God talked. He talked back. God liked Abraham so much He established a promise with him. Abraham built his future on that promise, and God was so pleased that many centuries later Abraham's future delivered Hope. World Hope.

In this story God declares He will obliterate a city off the face of the planet. This didn't sit well with Abraham. So, he did the unthinkable. He challenged God. He did so respectfully, but he still challenged God. Listen in, as the showdown begins.

> The men turned away and went toward Sodom, but Abraham remained standing before the LORD. Then Abraham approached him and said: "Will you sweep away the righteous with the wicked? What if there are fifty righteous people in the city? Will you really sweep it away and not spare the place for the sake of the fifty righteous people in it?
>
> Far be it from you to do such a thing—to kill the righteous with the wicked, treating the righteous and the wicked alike. Far be it from you! Will not the Judge of all the earth do right?"
>
> The Lord said, "If I find fifty righteous people in the city of Sodom, I will spare the whole place for their sake."
>
> Then Abraham spoke up again: "Now that I have been so bold as to speak to the Lord, though I am nothing but dust and ashes, what if the number of the righteous is five less than fifty? Will you destroy the whole city because of five people?"
>
> "If I find forty-five there," he said, "I will not destroy it."
>
> (Genesis 18:22-28)

The amazing Abraham took it all the way down to ten. He pushed it and pushed it. The tension of the moment was palpable. I could hardly keep reading. I kept thinking God would do the smote thing. However, He silently walks away.

> When the LORD had finished speaking with Abraham,
> he left, and Abraham returned home. (Genesis 18:33)

PEELING BACK THE LAYERS

I love this story. You feel the rising drama. You see Abraham taking each inch of real estate. He's bantering with God! This, then, is prayer. *Prayer is a gutsy conversation you have with God.*

> *Prayer is a gutsy conversation.*

There are many layers to it. In this story you see all the layers.

Layer 1

"Then Abraham approached." The best approach to God is face to face. God wants you to take a step toward Him. God wants you to move in His direction. He wants to hear what you're going to say. He wants to know what's on your mind. He wants to engage you. The best approach is the move to resolutely *approach.* I first prayed in earnest to God when I was 12. I wanted to go to Boy Scout Camp, but the year before my dad said "*no.*" When my big burly dad said no, the talk was over. So, I tentatively approached God with *the camp prayer.* The next day my dad came into my room. His hulking frame filled the doorway. He never came into my room. I gulped. He said, *"You can go to camp"* and left. I learned prayer worked, in that moment of incredulity. I can still hear his heavy footsteps on the creaky stairs as God was answering my Troop 251 prayer face to face.

Layer 2

The best way to ask is to ask the obvious. God knows your

mind and what you're thinking about. All Abraham does is to state the obvious. "If there are 50 righteous people in the city are you going to destroy everything and take out the righteous people; the good people with the bad people? It just doesn't seem right. How could you do something like that?" He states the *obvious*. So often we get tongue-tied. We think there's more to explain to God than there really is. Just tell Him the obvious. What you see is what you talk about. What you feel is what you talk about.

Layer 3

Always remember God is fair. Notice what Abraham does by saying:

"Far be it from you! Will not the Judge of all the earth do right?"

(Genesis 18:25)

God ordered the universe according to His specifications. God cares about every detail of our lives. He cares about the moment. He cares about the feeling you have *right now*. He cares about the feeling you had when you got up this morning. Rest in the fact that God is *fair and will ultimately be fair even when you don't see it today*.

Layer 4

The best way to be humble is not to bumble. Humility doesn't mean falling down and making yourself look incompetent before God. It means seeing yourself in proper perspective. Abraham approached God, stated the obvious, knew God would be fair, and humbled himself saying:

"Now that I have been so bold as to speak to the Lord, though I am nothing but dust and ashes..."
(Genesis 18:27)

Humility doesn't mean thinking less of yourself. Humility just means thinking of yourself *less*. In Abraham's humility, he doesn't bumble. In his humility, he doesn't lose track of where he's going. He's able to go toe-to-toe with God with gracious motivation.

Layer 5

The best focus is no hocus-pocus. By the time Abraham gets down to interceding for 40 good guys, it's as obvious as Egypt and pyramids where he's going with his numeric shake and bake. Nevertheless, he keeps his focus. He's not manipulating in any way, shape, or form. The no chicanery zone is tight. Have you tried to manipulate God in prayer? You know what I'm talking about. It's when you say things like, *God if you'll do this for me, I'll do this for you.* God shakes His head and wonders when you'll get real. He wants us to stay focused. No manipulation, no hocus-pocus.

"What the world longs for from the Christian faith is the witness of men and women daring enough to be different, humble enough to make mistakes, wild enough to be burnt in the fire of love, real enough to make others see how unreal they are." [3]

Layer 6

The best way to push it is to relentlessly push it. Abraham keeps pushing God, "What if there are 30 people? What if there are 20 people?" He keeps pushing it. And I believe, with all my heart, God wants us to push it.

Jesus tells a story about an unjust judge who didn't care about God or anyone, but a woman is in his face begging for justice. She's everywhere he turns, asking the same question over and over. She wears him out. Finally, he throws his arms up in frustration and blurts, *This woman is driving me crazy! I'm going to give her what she wants just so I don't have to be bothered with her anymore!* And Jesus looks at the crowd and asks,

"If that's the way the unjust judge responds to someone who's pushing it and pushing it, how much more is God going to respond to you when you push it." (Luke 18:1-7 author's translation)

God wants us to relentlessly push it not because it changes *Him*, but because it begins to change *us*. It defines us. It sifts us out. It helps us to evaluate motives. It helps us to know if we really want something wholeheartedly. It helps us to state transparent desire.

Layer 7

When peeling back the layers of prayer, another vital principle to remember is that *the best question is your last question*. Abraham finally gets there and says, *"May the Lord not be angry, but let me speak just once more."* He knows he's at the last question. The last question is always the best question because it's the question you wanted to ask God at the beginning but for some reason you were afraid. When you finally bring that trembling question out, from behind your back, you and God have had a meeting at the heart level.

WHAT I KNOW ABOUT PRAYER

My best prayers are gut level prayers.

Sometimes I don't have words. I have gut-level groans I know. Prayer has less to do about vocabulary and more to do about feelings. God wants to engage with the big deals and the little deals. He *loves* hearing your gut-level reactions to life's needs.

Prayer is an effective strategy any time, any place.

I pray on the subway when I'm in New York. I pray when I'm walking. Sometimes God says "yes." Sometimes He says "no." Yet other times He says "wait" or "grow." Prayer is where I find myself again and again when I'm lost. Prayer is the greatest resource we have. It is free and unlimited in scope. You can pray for somebody right now on the other side of the world. And you can say grace as you have your lunch today. Prayer reminds us who we belong to and where we're going. God knows what we need even before we pray, but He still loves to hear us pray. We mostly think about prayer as a way of getting things, but the biblical principle is so much more about *becoming* something because of the intimacy we develop with God. It's about being with Him and being changed because we are with Him.

One more thing I know is this—you may be the answer to somebody's prayer.

Not long ago, I was in New York walking on 8th Avenue near 45th Street.

Suddenly, a woman wearing a blue top and denim shorts approached me and said, "Would you like to go out?"

"Excuse me?" I said, unsure of what I just heard.

"Would you like to go out?" she repeated.

Befuddled in the moment, I blurted out the only thing that would come to my mind. "I don't do that." I'm pretty sure that was the right answer.

"Oh, I'm sorry," she said sheepishly.

"You should go to church!" I half-shouted as she walked away. I turned and walked into a store to buy a Swiss Army Knife. But I couldn't shake her from my mind.

A few minutes later, as I was leaving the store, I felt queasy.

"You blew that off," I sensed God saying to me. "You just walked away. You could have spent another two minutes talking to her. You spent 10 minutes in the store getting a Swiss Army knife. That's a person; a human being made in My image.

I kept hearing words of infinite wisdom in my head. I *had* conveniently walked away. *"Go to church!"* Yeah, that'll do the trick. I'm sure she'll turn her life around by the first pitch tonight, in the Bronx.

I knew what I had to do. I started walking a couple of blocks north on 8th Avenue and at 48th Street, I saw her. She was nose-deep in some kind of brochure. She wore a bewildered look. Out of the corner of my eye I noticed a person handing out church brochures. Think about this for a moment. Just a few minutes ago she heard my words, and now she's reading church info. Think someone was trying to get her attention?

"Hi," I said. She looked up. "You know, you really, really should think about going to church. I think you know better than this."

"Yes," she nodded. Sad, empty eyes told her story. This was her moment. Her next move changes everything.

My gut was telling me one other thing. I think that somewhere, maybe that morning or maybe the night before, that girl's mother prayed for her wayward daughter. Or maybe it was her sister who felt compelled to pray. Or perhaps her brother said, "Help my sister. I love her. She needs to know You." *I was the answer to somebody's prayer that day.* So often we think it's all about asking God for something for us. You never know who might be waiting for God to send you.

WHEN THERE ARE NO WORDS

Here's what you need to remember when life has you on your knees with confusion raining down and worry permeating your soul.

> "In the same way, the Spirit helps us in our weakness. We do not know what we ought to pray for, but the Spirit himself intercedes for us with groans that words cannot express." (Romans 8:26)

Don't we often live at the intersection of sweat and tears? We don't know how to pray. We can't harness words to describe the vexation. Our minds are a ratatouille of contusions, hopes, longings, dreams and failures. We flail at concepts and categories. Then Paul drops a bombshell. He presents us with the *groaning principle*. We are not to drown in our emotional stew—God *Himself* prays for us. Does that fit in your brain? He knows the details of your next move. When you are falling He has you in His grip.

Worried about not knowing how to pray? Take heart. Take a breath. God is praying for you as you shift gears into your next decisive move.

DEEPER MOVES

In a *Christianity Today* article, Philip Yancey writes:

> "Life is not a problem to be solved, but a mystery to be lived. Prayer offers no ironclad guarantees — just the certain promise that we need not live that mystery alone." [5]

In his book, *Prayer*, Yancey describes three stages of prayer.

The first stage he calls *Child-like Prayer*. This is when you say, *God I need this; I'm hoping for this.* It's when you cry out in simplicity to God and you do what Abraham did where he merely stated the obvious. Children live and move in the present moment. They're living out their lives in the obvious. No wonder Jesus used an illustration about children when trying to describe how we are to gain Altitude with God.

The second stage Yancey calls *Keeping Company with God*. We don't tend to use that phrase much any more because we're flying around maxing out our days. But I can remember a time when people used that phrase a lot. *I will keep her company. I will keep you company.*

I was once greatly surprised when an African pastor at a leadership conference did something that, for me, was unusual. After exchanging pleasantries I told him it was nice talking to him and started to quickly walk away to go to my car for something. I'm always going somewhere for something. He stopped me in my tracks saying, "I will walk with you." He said it very calmly with large eyes looking into my soul. Then together we walked slowly continuing our conversation to the far reaches of the parking lot and back. He had turned a parking lot into a cathedral because he just wanted to keep company with me. To keep company with God, walk slowly with Him. Let Him search your heart when there's nothing else going on. There's no game. There's no show. There's no place you have to get to. There aren't three places you've got to be tomorrow. It's just you and God, in the tender moment.

The third stage Yancey calls *Submission*. It's what I call, *I'm not gonna let you down*. It's simply saying, "God I'm here, and if You need me or if You choose me to accomplish something or to stand in the gap for someone, I'm here. I know I work for You. Let me know what's next."

I once asked a man from Togo, West Africa, *"What's your dream?"* He was leading a church in a village. The village was past the boonies. As if he'd rehearsed it for days, he stated matter-of-factly, *"To have clean water in my village. Will you help me?"* I scored a zero—a *zero* on the Air Force mechanical aptitude scale. Why would God pick me to help on a water project? I said I would try. I made some moves and ended up in Togo two years later. I brought a team of people brimming with mechanical and geological aptitude. They drilled a well. I watched. Today there are 50 wells. 10,000 people have water, jobs, gardens, and hope. [6] I really believe *I'm not gonna let you down* is the best way to live out prayer. Michel Soka Ahossey was praying for a long time. God answered his prayers through *I'm not gonna let you down.*

In his chapter *What to Pray For* Yancey writes, "Unanswered prayers and unanswered questions about God and physical healing can leave us feeling confused and mute about the requests we present. What exactly should we pray for? From interviews with suffering people and ordinary pray-ers, from the experience of caregivers, chaplains, and helpers, I have gathered the following guidelines on prayer. These prayers we can count on, and pray with confidence." [7]

Yancey delineates some prayer guidelines. [8]

Pray about your heart's desire.

Pray about what you want at the deepest level. Pray something wells up inside your heart you will be thrilled to clutch. God put a desire inside you only you can gain Altitude with. Find it. Live it. Accomplish it.

Pray about your laments.

I call these your complaints. It's nothing new to God that we complain. It's nothing new to God that we have issues. Go to God with your issues. Go to God with your complaints. All throughout the Bible, people are complaining to God about things. One of your best prayers can be an honest complaint.

Pray to confess.

When you know you did or said something wrong, or perhaps when you know you thought something wrong about someone, make a move.

"If we confess our sins, he is faithful and just and will forgive us our sins..." (1 John 1:9)

Confession is a prayer God is always going to hear. He hears and forgives. Done deal.

Pray please show up.

Asking God to show up can be transformational. *Please show up in this boardroom. Please show up when I'm taking my exams, when I'm finishing school. Please show up at home because things at home are really hard right now. Please show up in this relationship. God, please show up on Sunday morning and say something about my next move.* When you ask God to show up, look for Him to show up.

Pray for faith.

God doesn't give us a printout at the beginning of each day so we know exactly what's going to happen and how it's going to work. Life will never be that way, but God says, "Trust Me. Have faith in Me."

And without faith it is impossible to please God, because anyone who comes to him must believe that he exists and that he rewards those who earnestly seek him. (Hebrews 11:6)

Faith is the action that energizes God. A prayer for faith is what gets God up in the morning. Make that prayer your next move to gain Altitude.

THE BIG THREE

Let me tell you about the three biggest prayers of my life. Each one defines a moment and creates the future.

A Dangerous Prayer

The first one was 37 years ago. I remember it quite vividly. I was in my apartment. I walked into the bathroom and looked in the mirror. As I was getting ready to shave, I saw my reflection in the mirror and this thought came to me: "You are so selfish. *You are so selfish.* You say you want to do the things God wants you to do. But most of the time it's, 'What's this going to do for Michael? How's this going to pay off for Michael?' You're out there kind-of doing ministry but part of you is covertly selfish. You demand things from God. You're making demands about everything, including marrying the perfect person." I was jolted by that revelation. My prayer that day was: "God, I will marry the person *You* want me to marry." Prayers like that could be placed on a pedestal as *bold* or *unselfish* but, the truth is, they can be dangerous. Because if you *really* mean the words, you'll have to be content with how God answers. In my case, I knew right away what God was going to do; He was going to bring me somebody who couldn't cook. And that's exactly what happened.

Selfishness aside, what God knew was that everything else in Gail's life was going to be *exactly* what He prescribed for the ensuing decades of my life. I don't know how He did that, but this amazing curly-haired woman, who materialized out of thin air, was everything *I* needed to achieve all God needed *us* to do. She chiseled my character with His hammer. She spoke truth into my life even when I'd try to block it. It turned out she was praying in quiet moments, "God, bring me a challenge." Talk about dangerous prayers! They don't get more dangerous than that. She was ready for Altitude with a guy who could barely fly a paper airplane!

That prayer move changed everything.

I Have a Place For You Here

The next biggest prayer was almost two decades ago. A church in the Northeast offered me a good job. It was a big church, a good church. They offered me more money than I thought was legal. It was a 30-40% raise, and they would take care of all kid costs. Ski trip? Done. High school retreat? Done. Mission trip? Done. There would be no out-of-pocket expenses for the kids. That was huge. And, as if that wasn't enough, they also threw an advance of retirement cash on the table and said, "Here, buy a house." *This was a big deal.* Gail and I just couldn't get our heads wrapped around it, though. We would pray about it yet couldn't get there. Disequilibrium ruled our hearts. We interviewed several times. We talked to everybody. I went on a staff retreat for a weekend. Still something held us back. *Stuckness was where we lived on this one.*

One Saturday morning, I went to my church. I walked to the front of the sanctuary and sat in the second pew. I got down on my knees and said, "Oh God, I can't make this decision." And if I ever heard the voice of God, I heard it right then. God whispered to me, "I have a place for you here." That was all He said. So we looked at that huge amount of money, the impending move, the forthcoming change in our lives, and said, *"We can't go. God said He has a place for us here."* I shudder to think about what we would have missed had we listened to the call of financial security rather than getting ready to make a move that would change the game.

Thy Will Be Done

I didn't want to write this one down, but God said, *"Write this one. This is it."* My third biggest prayer is to know and do His will.

Believe me, I am far from being a perfect person. I just want to know and do what He wants me to do. And I want to know what He wants Spring Branch to do. What does our next big run look like? What's our next assignment? If you haven't been praying that kind of prayer for yourself and the people you lead, you are missing out on one of God's greatest adventures. Are you ready for a dangerous prayer? Ask God to show you the area you most need to grow in as a leader or follower. Where do you need to grow? Where do you need to stretch? Where do you need to mature the most? Do you need to do some lamenting and get that out of the way first? *Ask God to meet you in the mirror.* Pray that prayer and I promise it'll bring your next move to your door. I believe God will show up and explain your move in any number of ways. It might happen on a Sunday morning. It might happen by somebody talking to you.

Or, God might whisper in your ear like He does to me sometimes.

I was in Saks Fifth Avenue not long ago. I always like to walk through the Men's Department. It's simply amazing. I usually do a big circle, look at all the Zegna and Corneliani, and then walk out. On my way out, however, I have to navigate through the cosmetics gauntlet. You can't walk two feet without somebody spritzing something on you, handing you a sample of something, or wiping some cream on you. There are dozens and dozens of these smiling sprayers. You're always having to weave your way through the labyrinth. I was in the maze forging my way towards Fifth Avenue when suddenly there she was. *Right in front of me.* I loved seeing this person on TV for a long time. She's not on TV much any more but there she was, right in front of me—Jane Pauley. Jane Pauley!

I just wanted to reach out and touch her. However, I froze in my tracks and watched her sail by. I happened to be standing like a mannequin in front of a perfume counter and the salesperson said, "Can I help you?" I said, "I just want to meet Jane." She dryly replied, "Everybody wants to meet Jane."

I'm never going to meet Jane. I almost did, but I'll probably never see her again. Oh, well. But I *can* banter with God on a daily basis. You can, too. You can be agonizingly honest with Him. You can lay out your hopes before Him. You can even complain to Him. You can *not say anything* and He reads the deepest cries of your heart. He wants to hear your voice.

Make your next move a gutsy conversation.

WHAT I KNOW ABOUT PRAYER

- My best prayers are gut level

- Prayer has less to do about words and more to do about feelings and/or the reality at hand

- God wants to engage with the big deals and the little deals

- Prayer is an effective strategy any time/any place

- God says Yes...No...and Wait, sometimes even Maybe...but you still have to wait

- Prayer is where I find myself again when I'm lost

- Prayer is where I connect my life to your life

- Prayer is the greatest resource we have, it is free and unlimited in scope

- Prayer reminds us who we belong to and where we're going

- God knows what we need even before we pray, but loves to hear us pray

- We mostly think about prayer as a way of getting things... but the biblical principle is so much more about becoming something because of the intimacy we develop with God...

- There is one more thing I know about prayer: You may be the answer to someone's prayer

Dear Michael,

I search your heart.

I know what lies in the deepest places.

I know what you try to hide in those little boxes you made and I know what you struggle to overcome. Not one of you receives a perfect life. The cycle repeats itself from one generation to the next. What you need more of is Me. What you need more of is seeing yourself and everyone else through My heart. You will dig less pits and have less falls if you just believe Me.

Life is a long series of events that are designed for your radical spiritual transformation. At a young age you're vulnerable and must depend on adults for radical wisdom. When that doesn't happen it sets you off wobbling and teeter-tottering toward confusion and emptiness. The ache most people feel inside, beginning about age 16, is from the absence of the radical spiritual moment when they were to be given their own set of transformational instructions. They begin to bypass Me, pursuing their own agendas, while accepting their ache as reality. Sometimes they ignore the ache and make believe it isn't there at all; always a major error. That's when people start constructing their own syncretistic beliefs and moral instructions, which become a labyrinth of existential assessments that eventually get one lost. These well intentioned efforts are tantamount to trying to write a magnificent play with a 3rd grade education. You'll get something and it may even be entertaining, but don't try to extract too much meaning from it, because there's no spiritual depth or emotional experience behind it.

It's that lack of depth that permeates most people's lives, just like it once smothered your life. There are two things that need to happen and you know what they are, because I've taught you this. First, a person must face their empty places and be honest about where they came from. I know that's the hardest part. It's an exquisitely thorny endeavor to be honest about what you are not. Once a thorough inventory has been accomplished, we move on to strategy two, shaping the future with the right set of radical insights and adventures. The insights lead to adventures and the adventures give you insights. That juxtaposition was one of My finest calculations.

Each day has its moments when you choose whether or not to be a new person. Each day I prompt you in radical spiritual experiences that transform your heart. Don't look for them all to be bigger than life, however. Most of the time they'll stare you in the face before you realize it's Me again. Most of the time when you think things are crazy or dicey or confusing or weird or too hard, it's just Me testing your Radical IQ.

You want to know more about your adventures, don't you? When do they show up? How do you know which ones to say yes to? They are spiritual choices which arrive in various disguises. You can leap beyond the safe curriculum any time you want. Truth be told, safe is never what it appears to be and never delivers what it promises. Just ask Me and I'll make sure the right adventure choice is there at the right time. Sometimes I'll push you into it.

You will be wounded, you will be heart-broken, you will shine, you will inhale the meaning of life and laugh. You will mourn and you will dance. In the end you will look intently into My eyes and know that for all time you were loved just for being you. You were enough for My journey. You were enough for My own radical adventure. You see I proved it all works. In its serendipitous, radical way it all works.

Always remember—whenever it seems crazy or dicey or confusing or weird or too hard, that's Me working with you—and we'll get there together. I make the moves with you.

Be gutsy. I like gutsy.

God

Air Traffic Control

1. When did you first know prayer worked? What was that *Boy Scout Camp* prayer?

_____

_____

_____

_____

2. What's most confusing and ambiguous about prayer for you now?

_____

_____

_____

_____

3. What prayer would you pray if you knew God would answer it in the next 5 minutes?

_____

_____

_____

_____

4. How could you be the answer to someone's prayer this week?

_____

_____

_____

5. How do you feel when God says *No* or *Wait* or *Grow*?

_____

_____

_____

6. Read *The Lord's Prayer* slowly (Matthew 6:9-13). What's been blowing right past you without much thought?

_____

_____

_____

Our Father, who art in heaven, hallowed be thy name.
Thy Kingdom come, thy will be done,
on earth as it is in heaven.
Give us this day our daily bread.
And forgive us our trespasses,
as we forgive those who trespass against us.
And lead us not into temptation, but deliver us from evil.
For thine is the kingdom, the power and the glory,
for ever and ever.

Flying Higher

Prayer: Does It Make Any Difference?, Philip Yancey (Zondervan)

Couples Who Pray: The Most Intimate Act Between a Man and a Woman, SQuire Rushnell and Louise DuArt (Thomas Nelson)

A Companion to Couples Who Pray, (8 Session Study Guide)
SQuire Rushnell, Louise DuArt & Michael Simone (House on the Vineyard)

Flight Log

My notes on Gutsy Conversation

_____

_____

_____

_____

_____

_____

_____

_____

_____

_____

_____

_____

_____

_____

_____

_____

_____

_____

_____

_____

Your Seventh Move

Answer the Right Questions

For a miracle,

take one shepherd's sheepskin, throw
In a pinch of now, a grain of long ago,
And a handful of tomorrow. Add by eye
A little chunk of ground, a piece of sky,

And it will happen. For miracles, gravitating
To earth, know just where people will be waiting,
And eagerly will find the right address
And tenant, even in a wilderness.

Joseph Brodsky
25.XII.1993

SOONER OR LATER you have to answer the right questions in life. We all do. From barrios to gated enclaves to kitchen tables, finding answers to life is the work of life. The right questions are goads for the soul. How much is enough? How much does hope cost? How can you afford your life? These are the questions the King will ask of you on a night when the angels sing.

And there were shepherds living out in the fields nearby, keeping watch over their flocks at night. An angel of the Lord appeared to them, and the glory of the Lord shone around them, and they were terrified. But the angel said to them, "Do not be afraid. I bring you good news of great joy that will be for all the people. Today in the town of David a Savior has been born to you; he is Christ the Lord. This will be a sign to you: You will find a baby wrapped in cloths and lying in a manger."

Suddenly a great company of the heavenly host appeared with the angel, praising God and saying, "Glory to God in the highest, and on earth peace to men on whom his favor rests."

When the angels had left them and gone into heaven, the shepherds said to one another, "Let's go to Bethlehem and see this thing that has happened, which the Lord has told us about."

So they hurried off and found Mary and Joseph, and the baby, who was lying in the manger. When they had seen him, they spread the word concerning what had been told them about this child, and all who heard it were amazed at what the shepherds said to them. But Mary treasured up all these things and pondered them in her heart. The shepherds returned, glorifying and praising God for all the things they had heard and seen, which were just as they had been told. (Luke 2:8-20)

Many are struggling to make it day to day. Governments flex their muscles in a display of political power. The question seems to hang in the air. *Are we going to survive? Are we going to make it?* That was the world that Jesus was born into and it's not so different from the world that we seem to be in today. I love this passage from Luke and I love two short phrases in the passage: *"And they were terrified."* They were terrified. What in the world is going on now? What does this mean about my life? Am I going to have a life? Am I going to have a future? How can all these things be happening to me? I don't understand. And then there's the phrase just a few verses later. *"And all who heard it were amazed."* It's incredible the way life can surprise us, the way life can draw us into a mystery that goes beyond our ability to comprehend. And suddenly we're amazed and overwhelmed, "You mean this is the life I get to be a part of? This is the life I get to live? I can almost see a future and a hope from here." And so somehow we live between terrified and amazed.

Jackie Gingrich Cushman wrote in her column, *Christmas Joy I Can Believe In—*

> "It's Christmas week, school is out, relatives are in town and my shopping is not done. My cards are not out, my house is not clean, and I am feeling undone. The pine roping I bought two weeks ago is still curled up in my carport, and I have yet to find my mailbox decorations. Christmas perfection is rapidly turning into a hallucination." [1]

And she's right. We want Christmas perfection. But it's like a hallucination. It's like something we reach out for only to see it evaporate into thin air. We live somewhere between being terrified and amazed. Terrified—*Are we going to get it all done?* How's it going to be Christmas? We're not ready yet! It's so close and we are so far away. And yet it chugs like a charging, glowering locomotive, wheels riding steel into our dreams, pegging the meter. Then she waxes poetic and eloquent. In this brilliant statement she captures everything, *"It requires constant vigilance to remind myself that Christmas is not about where and how but whom."* [2] Christmas is not about where and how but whom. She is dreaming about Christmas and almost getting there. She's dreaming about all her preparations and she's not quite there. She can't quite reach the pinnacle. Then she remembers eight graceful words—*It's not about how and where but whom.*

THE FIRST QUESTION

We all have Christmas dreams. Let's go beyond dreams. Let's

go right into the heart of Christmas because you must answer three questions between terror and amazement. It's the only way to make a move toward Christmas. Imagine walking into a Royal Court. Imagine being in the presence of Divine Royalty. The King will ask you the first question and it is always this, *How much is enough in the life you live? How much is enough?*

I love baseball and I had a fantastic 2008 baseball summer. *I had an incredible baseball summer.* It started with the All-Star Game in New York City, the last All-Star game at Old Yankee Stadium. The longest All-Star game ever. I sat there for every glorious moment of 15 innings of baseball pageantry. It was mesmerizing, it was far beyond what I'd hoped for, and I was there. Then I toured New Yankee Stadium. I was on the field! Then I got to sit right up close to the field at the 12th to the last game at Old Yankee Stadium. I could almost reach out and touch Alex Rodriguez. And so, *I had an incredible baseball summer.* After such wonderfulness I thought, *OK, Michael, now you have been to two World Series, you have been to two All-Star games, you have toured New Yankee Stadium, you have been to Cooperstown, you met Mickey Mantle personally, it's time to say enough is enough and not ask for anything else when it comes to baseball for the rest of your life. Just be satisfied for what you've been given in your lifetime.* And then, I get an e-mail, "Did you hear that they're going to do some pre-season games at New Yankee Stadium and they're rolling back prices to the 1920's so you can sit in the bleachers for 25 cents?" And I said, *"I want that! I am there!"*

That's what a problem this is in my life. I need help! I am crying out for help! Somebody please help me! I don't know what to do! You see, enough is never enough if you base *enough* on human desire. In human desire enough is about consumption.

How much can I have? How much can I want? But change the equation. Tweak it just a bit. Let it not be about consumption but about compassion and timing and it all changes. *For enough is always enough when you know that whatever you have was meant to be given away at the right time in the right place for the right reasons.* Whenever you do that enough is the sum total of your heart being in the right place. And that is always enough. It's always enough when your heart is in the right place.

Take the innkeeper for instance, you could look at him and say he didn't do enough! He should have made room for them! He should've gone far beyond baseline customer service to take these two in for the night. This is a woman who's about to have a baby! But if you say *he didn't do enough* you miss the mystery. You must see the mystery of God in a manger and know He needed a feed trough that night. What would the story be without the manger? You see, the innkeeper gave *what he had.* He had a barn. He gave it. *So enough was fulfilled in compassion and timing.* If you answer the King, enough is never enough. He will know you lack understanding and you only think about desire and consumption. But if you answer the King, *enough is when I have given my heart for the right reason in the right place,* He will know you are close to knowing the truth that sets you free. *Enough is when I have given my heart for the right reason in the right place.*

THE SECOND QUESTION

How much does hope cost?

The King will ask you a second question. *How much does hope cost?*

For days I hoped my box would arrive. I hoped my package would arrive from New York City. I hoped, and I hoped, but it didn't arrive.

A few years ago I went to my 40th high school reunion. Gail and I journeyed back to days of old in New Jersey. Midland Park High School, class of 1968. I walked into a dimly lit restaurant. There they were, Joe, Andy, Al, Bob, Chuck. All the football players, all the running backs looked like they should be the bulky defensive line for any NFL team. I was on the track team. Today, we can't run around the building without the rescue squad standing by. Then there's the basketball team. These are guys who could *sky* and *slam*. I was about to have the greatest moment in my life. One of my closest friends had made the All-State basketball team. He was a terrific player. He could jam, he could make the outside shot. He had this shot from the corner. There was hardly an arc on the ball, and BAM! It would go in just about every time. He was 6'2". Everyone loved him. I went over and stood next to Ric at the reunion and, finally, I was taller than him. I looked down on him. It was one of the greatest moments of my sports career.

After the reunion we went to New York City. We stayed at the Sheraton Hotel. It is one of the biggest hotels in New York. It's an international hotel. People stay there from all over the world. We decided to ship some things home rather than schlep them through the airport. So, I go down to the Business Center at the Sheraton Hotel on Seventh Avenue, one of the biggest international hotels in New York. And I go to the Business Center and I figure I can do *business* here because that's what it says, *Business Center*. I have assorted items to put in a box and I meet a guy named Marcus. I said to Marcus, "I want to ship this stuff home." He said, "That's not a problem." I said, "Okay, I have this picture of Yankee Stadium my brother gave me, I've got this Yankee mug I bought at Macy's for 20% off. I have a few other items here, a sweatshirt I don't want to pack in my suitcase. Can we pack it all in a box and ship it home? He said, "Not a problem, Mr. Simone." So, he put everything in the box, and I said, "Are we good to go Marcus?" He said, "We are good to go." Eleven bucks was the price of hope as in *if I pay $11.00 I hope the box will travel the 350 miles to Virginia Beach.* I gave him $11 and said, "Are we good to go, Marcus?" He said, "Just fill out this paperwork for FedEx and it'll be fine." I filled out the paperwork and I said, "Are we good to go Marcus?" He said, "We are good to go."

That box disappeared for weeks. Day after day went by and my wife kept asking me about the box. I got more and more frustrated. After a week went by and we sprinted into another week, I called the Sheraton in New York, one of the biggest international hotels in New York, where people come from all over the world to stay. It has a Business Center and a guy named Marcus works there. So, I got Marcus on the phone and said, "Marcus, this is Mr. Simone. Do you remember me?" He said, "No." I said, "Remember we put the Yankee picture in the box." He said, "Oh yeah! I'm glad you called. The box is right here." I said, "Marcus, what's the deal." He said, "Well, you didn't give me enough money." A video tape of *that'll be $11.00* played in my head. I was home hoping in vain for a box still in New York City, because eleven bucks for hope wasn't enough.

You see hope always costs everything, but it is never sufficient. And so, when the King asks, *"How much does hope cost?"* You must be ready to answer.

For centuries people hoped for some answer to life. For centuries people hoped that there was more to life than just life. And their hopes piled up and piled up until they would reach the heavens. Promises came and were written down and remembered from generation to generation.

> Therefore the Lord himself will give you a sign: The virgin will be with child and will give birth to a son, and will call him Immanuel. God with us. (Isaiah 7:14)
> See, your king comes to you, righteous and having salvation, gentle and riding on a donkey, on a colt, the foal of a donkey. (Zechariah 9:9)

A king doesn't ride a quasi-majestic donkey. But it's a picture of something that would happen long into the future when Jesus would ride into Jerusalem, at the beginning of the week where He ends up giving His life for us.

> "But you, Bethlehem Ephrathah, though you are small among the clans of Judah, out of you will come for me one who will be ruler over Israel, whose origins are from of old, from ancient times. (Micah 5:2)

There it is. Bethlehem. The hopes of many were poured out in tears, in songs, in dreams, in faith. Then one ordinary day, a young girl received an angelic word, placing her life in God's hands. It was all she had to give. All her hopes came down to that one moment, and in the giving of everything hope seemed to be satisfied for a flickering moment. But it wasn't. Because if it depended on her will and her own work, it still would not be enough.

So the King asks, "How much does hope cost?" And you are ready to answer the King, "Hope always costs everything I have, but it is never enough."

THE THIRD QUESTION

And then the King says, "There's one more question. How can you afford to live the fullness of your days?" It is then you must have great presence of mind. It is then you must start to think expansively, because you can only afford your days if you see what others do not always see.

Let me tell you a story about seeing. One of my great dreams was to go to the Louvre to see the Mona Lisa. I'd seen her picture for decades. I'd heard the stories, and studied about Leonardo da Vinci, but I wanted to see her up close and personal. I wanted to see her, as it were, *face to face*. And so in 2009, we took a trip to Paris and spent a week there. We had one day to spend at the Louvre and I looked forward to that colorful day. The day came. We walked through the grand hallways and finally I came to that spot where the sign said Mona Lisa. I went into a great room. At the far end there she was. I could barely make her out but there she was. Hundreds and hundreds of people were funneling down to get right in front of her. I stepped into the line. I got up close and looked her right in the eye. She looked me right in the eye. I looked at her smile. I just couldn't take my eyes off of her. Then something happened, I started to think in a different way. I started to think about a different way of seeing. And I began to wonder, *Everybody comes from all over the world to see this woman. What is it that Mona Lisa sees all day long from her vantage point in this great room? What does Mona Lisa see?* And so I turned around and tried to have her eyes and imagine what she saw, what she looked at all day long.

Let me show you what she sees. Right across from her is the largest painting in the Louvre. It was taken out of Italy centuries ago. To get it out of whatever room it was in they had to cut it in half to just move it. When they got to France they had to put it back together. The Italians later on said they didn't want it to have to be taken apart again so you can just keep it. You keep this painting. This is the painting of Jesus at the wedding of Cana, where He did His first miracle. I'm not so sure it was His first miracle. But there He is, the centerpiece of the picture. Your eye is drawn to Him. There's a halo around His head and everybody is having a great time at this wedding because Jesus is there. He's taking care of all refreshment details. Water to wine! Everything is good again.

And then I thought, *What is it she sees if she turns to the right?* And you turn to the right and you see Jesus as a baby with His mother and there are other pictures of Jesus as a baby. Jesus with Mary and Joseph and Jesus in the manger and then you start to look around and you see pictures of Jesus in His life and then you start to see Jesus carrying a cross. You look around again and you see Jesus with a crown of thorns and suddenly you realize what Mona Lisa sees all day long is the life of Jesus spread out in panoramic form around her. She sees Him doing miracles. She sees Him as a baby. She sees Him giving His life away. Mona Lisa sees in a way hardly anybody sees when they go into that room. *Mona Lisa sees Jesus.* She sees Him every day and all the time. He surrounds her. *You must see what Mona Lisa sees to gain Altitude.*

The King asked you, *How much is enough?* You responded, *Enough is always enough when you give your heart for the right reasons in the right place.*

The King asked you, *How much does hope cost?* You responded, *Hope always costs everything I have. But it is never enough.* Now the King finally asks you, *Then how can you afford your days? How can you afford your own life?* He asks because He wants to know if you can truly see who He is. At that moment you must see what others do not always see and answer, *I can't afford it. But I have seen the price paid for me. It requires constant vigilance to remind myself that Christmas is not about where and how...but whom.*

Then these words will ring in your ears and your eyes will be opened—

> "Hail the heav'n-born Prince of Peace!
> Hail the Sun of Righteousness!
> Light and life to all He brings,
> Ris'n with healing in His Wings.
> Mild He lays His Glory by,
> Born that man no more may die;
> Born to raise the sons of earth;
> born to give them second birth.
> Hark! the herald angels sing,
> Glory to the New-born king!" [3]

The Great King will smile.
He will reach out His hands to you.
In that magnificent moment you will know Christmas.

How much is enough? How much does hope cost? How can you afford it? These are the right questions of one night with the King. And all of the Altitude answers forever and always are found in Whom.

Dear Michael,

When you turned to Me, over forty years ago, you didn't think I'd answer you. You were desperately seeking something and it turned out to be Me. All of your searching ended in one puzzling plea for change. I zapped your heart under a bright night sky. You can still see the trail of light illuminating your mind. You finally blinked and I changed you. It is better to say I began to change you. I'm still at that work today. You were changed and you are changing. You must continue to change. You must move to grow.

Spiritual and personal transformation are so very tightly connected and yet it's important to remember that they are distinctly different. I didn't say they exist separately, just that there are distinctive qualities to each. Spiritual change comes from knowing Christ. He teaches you by the Spirit what you need to know and do with your life. This is your calling, your purpose, to be like Him. You are led into on earth as it is in heaven in spiritual transformation. Personal transformation is when you learn about hurtful behaviors and attitudes pressed into you by family or society and you decide to lay them aside. The Holy Spirit presides over both transformations and connects both, but you have to choose to let go of things that are holding you back from relational integrity. If you attend a Bible study and get angry at someone right afterward, that's an indication of the difference. If you want to show love and yet you hold back, again there's something needing your attention. You must make your move to work on this the rest of your life. It is the dilemma of this world.

However, you can grow and mature toward the ruthless pursuit of melding transparent faith and life challenges together. This is the wonder of crafting a spiritual legacy.

Significance happens when you begin to let go of your demands. When you loosen your grip on your stuff and see people the way I see them. I see them redemptively. I see them worthy of great sacrifice. I cherish them. I want them all to come to Me. When you plan and pray and sacrifice for others you write a legacy of the soul. This legacy is the most powerful script of all your journeys. It tells the tale of your dreams and what you were willing to move mountains for. It is your passion and humility wrapped in one package given as a spectacular gift to the next generation. The seed of your significance was planted by Christ. He rained grace upon it and tended it. He pruned it. Your significance is what we are growing together serenaded by Spirit thunder claps you only hear when you are very still.

So keep watch. Keep bringing faith to each day. Know Me in brokenness. Learn from sideways answers and from junctions that shatter the old and create the new. Hear the roar of forgiveness. Embrace significance. Feel the tinkering of My Spirit in every minute. Blink, and you will see it all.

You will move mountains when you answer the right questions.

God

Air Traffic Control

1. What was your best Christmas present as a child, and why?

_____

_____

_____

_____

2. What was your saddest Christmas moment or season? Where were you and what happened?

_____

_____

_____

_____

3. Describe the Christmas traditions in your family growing up. Have they stayed the same or changed?

_____

_____

_____

_____

4. Which of the three questions is most poignant for you? Why?

_____

_____

_____

_____

5. When did you pay an amount for *hope* and it wasn't enough?

_____

_____

_____

_____

6. What spiritual legacy are you crafting? If significance happens when you let go of your demands, what demand do you need to loosen your grip on?

_____

_____

_____

_____

_____

Flying Higher

Building Below the Waterline: Shoring Up the Foundations of Leadership, Gordon MacDonald (Hendrickson)

The Great Divorce, C. S. Lewis (HarperSanFrancisco)

A Christmas Carol, Charles Dickens (Dover Publications, Inc.)

Christmas Stories: Heartwarming Classics of Angels, A Manger, and The Birth of Hope, Max Lucado (Thomas Nelson)

Flight Log

My notes on Answer the Right Questions

_____

_____

_____

_____

_____

_____

_____

_____

_____

_____

_____

_____

_____

_____

_____

_____

_____

_____

_____

_____

_____

_____

Your Eighth Move

Know Who You Are...
Know Where You're Going

But you are

the only person alive
who has sole custody of your life.
Your particular life. Your entire life.
Not just your life at a desk,
or your life on the bus,
or in the car, or at the computer.
Not just the life of your mind,
But the life of your heart.
Not just your bank account, but your soul.
People don't talk about the soul
very much anymore.
It's so much easier to write a resume
than to craft a spirit.

Anna Quindlen
A Short Guide to a Happy Life

YOU CAN LIVE TO SURVIVE. You can live to experience excitement. You can live for the hope of a good retirement. You can live for a lot of reasons, but the most important of all is to *know who you are and to know where you're going.*

Pop-culture physicist Michio Kaku is a professor of theoretical physics at the City College of New York and he makes bold sweeping predictions about the future. He says, *"By 2020, the word computer will have vanished from the English language. We'll have millions of chips in all of our possessions: furniture, cars, appliances, clothes. We'll simply turn things on. When you need to see a doctor, you'll talk to a wall in your home and an animated artificially intelligent doctor will appear. The Internet will be in your contact lens. You will blink and you will go online. We'll become a fully globalized civilization by 2100. The planetary language will be English."* [1] So much for *cómo está usted* and my six years of studying Spanish. Dr. Kaku is incredibly visionary regarding his predictions. But when it comes to understanding who we are and where we're going it's quite a different story. He stated in an interview, *"To understand the universe, physicists first need to figure out what it's made of. We had to rewrite every textbook because 10 years ago they all said the universe is mainly made out of atoms. We now know that's wrong. In reality, atoms make up only 4% of the universe. The other 96% consists of dark matter and dark energy, two mysterious substances about which very little is known."* [2] And so, a very brilliant scientist makes sweeping predictions and still can't explain *who we really are or where we really came from.*

While it's interesting to speculate about the future, at the end of the day there's so much more to learn about the universe in which we have our zip code. Maybe we need to move beyond science and philosophical debate. To know who you are and know where you're going is a bigger issue than the physical universe question. The Bible says just that. There are rumors of a place beyond the stars. There are rumors of paradise. To look for answers to who you are and where you're going you'll ultimately have to accelerate beyond what is available on a day-to-day basis. As technologically sophisticated as the world is, some days it just doesn't quite get us where we need to go.

I was going on a trip recently and, being helpful, a friend gave me his GPS system to take with me to plug into my rental car. He said, "I've prepared this for you and I've put in all the places you're going to go so all you have to do is push this button and everything will work and you'll know exactly where you have to go. The machine will just tell you." I got to my destination and I plugged it in and pushed the button and heard these words, "At the end of the road take the ferry and then 2-step with me, you dig? Turn around when possible and keep it jig, you dig?" I'm listening to Snoop Dogg on the GPS? What in my world is going on? I prefer a more soothing instructional voice when driving. I changed the setting to the nice English woman.

I need to know who I am and where I'm going beyond technology. I need to know more than just where my body is and where it's going. I need to know where my soul is and where it's going.

JESUS PREDICTED THE FUTURE

It's 33 A.D. Springtime. Birds are singing. The sun is rising on a new universe.

> Early on the first day of the week, while it was still dark, Mary Magdalene went to the tomb and saw that the stone had been removed from the entrance. So she came running to Simon Peter and the other disciple, the one Jesus loved, and said, "They have taken the Lord out of the tomb, and we don't know where they have put him!"
>
> So, Peter and the other disciple started for the tomb. Both were running, but the other disciple outran Peter and reached the tomb first. He bent over and looked in at the strips of linen lying there but did not go in. Then Simon Peter, who was behind him, arrived and went into the tomb. He saw the strips of linen lying there, as well as the burial cloth that had been around Jesus' head. The cloth was folded up by itself, separate from the linen. Finally the other disciple, who had reached the tomb first, also went inside. He saw and believed.
>
> Jesus did many other miraculous signs in the presence of his disciples, which are not recorded in this book. But these are written that you may believe that Jesus is the Christ, the Son of God, and that by believing you may have life in his name.
>
> (John 20:1-8, 30-31)

Jesus predicted the future. He proffered that the universe was created by tiny particles called love. In the middle of the first century, Paul explained who you are and where you're going.

> He is the image of the invisible God, the firstborn over all creation.   (Colossians 1:15)

Paul is writing, to his friends, about the universe. You've heard of the truth. You know the truth. You've experienced the truth. Now you are building your lives upon that truth. *You know who you are and you know where you're going.* Jesus is the image of the invisible God. He holds everything together— everything God wanted to show you, everything He wanted to teach you, everything He wanted to reveal to you is in Jesus Christ. To know who you are and where you're going, *you must know who Christ is and where He came from.*

GOD IN TIMES SQUARE

Jesus keeps showing up century after century. There are debates like those surrounding The Shroud of Turin. There are philosophical Broadway shows like *Freud's Last Session* and *Godspell.* There are movies like *Leap of Faith* or *Simon Burch* and songs like *Jesus Take the Wheel.* There are a myriad of paintings that depict Him. He keeps showing up. He showed up April 9, 2012, on the cover of Newsweek. They placed him in Times Square with the crown of thorns still on his head. Tina Brown, the editor-in-chief wrote in her column on page 4 these words:

"Jesus was a lone, wandering preacher with a small knot of followers. His message was radical. Leave your family, give away all you own, and devote yourself selflessly to God—which meant loving not only one's neighbors, but also one's enemies. He was adamantly apolitical even to the point of refusing to defend himself at his own trial." [3]

And then she asks a very weighty question.

"So, how did we get to a point where the message of Christianity in America has drifted so far from Jesus?" [4]

It's a good question. In the article *The Forgotten Jesus*, Andrew Sullivan writes about a founding father:

"I am a real Christian," Jefferson insisted against the fundamentalists and clerics of his time. "That is to say, a disciple of the doctrines of Jesus." Sullivan writes, "Whether or not you believe, as I do, in Jesus' divinity and resurrection-and in the importance of celebrating both on Easter Sunday- Jefferson's point is crucially important. Because it was Jesus' point. What does it matter how strictly you proclaim your belief in various doctrines if you do not live as these doctrines demand?" [5]

Tina Brown *is* asking the key question.

"So how did we get to the point where the message of Christianity in America has drifted so far from Jesus?" [6]

And then Newsweek becomes almost biblical—

"The thirst for God is still there. How could it not be, when the profoundest human questions—Why does the universe exist rather than nothing? How did humanity come to be on this remote blue speck of a planet? What happens to us after death—remain as pressing and mysterious as they've always been?"[7]

To know who you are and where you're going, you must know who Christ is and where He came from. You see, Jesus predicted the future. He explained that the universe was created of tiny particles called love.

"No, the Father himself loves you because you have loved me and have believed that I came from God. I came from the Father and entered the world; now I am leaving the world and going back to the Father.

Then Jesus' disciples said, "Now you are speaking clearly and without figures of speech. Now we can see that you know all things and that you do not even need to have anyone ask you questions. This makes us believe that you came from God."

"You believe at last!" Jesus answered. "But a time is coming, and has come, when you will be scattered, each to his own home. You will leave me all alone. Yet I am not alone, for my Father is with me.

I have told you these things, so that in me you may have peace. In this world you will have trouble. But take heart! I have overcome the world." (John 16:27-33)

There have been rumors of a place beyond the universe, rumors of paradise. In Jesus Christ all those rumors fade away and they become the truth. The truth of life. The truth of how you can know who you are and where you're going. People have talked about Jesus across the centuries. Line by line, quote by quote.

Napoleon said, *"I know men and I tell you that Jesus Christ is no mere man. Between Him and every other person in the world there is no possible term of comparison."* [8]

H. G. Wells wrote, *"I am an historian, I am not a believer, but I must confess as a historian that this penniless preacher from Nazareth is irrevocably the very center of history. Jesus Christ is easily the most dominant figure in all history."* [9]

Larry King, ever the interviewer, posed this, *"I would like to ask him if he was indeed virgin born, because the answer to that question would define history."* [10]

Augustine, steeped in biblical history, wrote these words, *"Because God has made us for himself, our hearts are restless until they rest in Him."* [11]

FAITH IN FOOTBALL

Recently, I had words spoken into my life by the famous ex-NFL running back, Rocky Bleier. I was invited to the 67th Norfolk Sports Club dinner. I like sports. I like dinner. Win-win. I had never heard of Bleier (I'm a Giants fan), but his story had me on the edge of my seat. It amazed me. It humbled me. He was on the 1966 national championship team at Notre Dame. He was captain of that team in 1968. He was drafted by the Pittsburgh Steelers in 1968 in the 16th round. He was almost a sports afterthought. But he made the team and in 1969 he received his first fan mail—it was a letter from Uncle Sam. Uncle Sam wanted him to go to Vietnam.

He left the team and answered the call. On August 20, 1969, in Chu Lai, he was shot in the left thigh and also that same day stepped on a grenade and blew up his foot. Shrapnel embedded itself in his leg. He was a mess in the hospital at Da Nang. The thought he would never play football again dogged him. But the owner of the Steelers wanted him back, and the team gave him the chance to come back. He worked hard. He rehabbed hard. He worked harder than anyone.

This courageous and honorable man of faith went back to play for the Steelers. He played behind Terry Bradshaw and next to Franco Harris. *He won four Super Bowl rings!* I approached him after dinner, not knowing if I could even get close to him, suddenly we were face to face. I said, "You inspired me tonight." And he looked at me with a twinkle in his eye and said, "I heard something the other day and I almost used it tonight, *'It's a sin to be good when God made you to be great.'* "I will carry those words with me to my grave." *It's a sin to be good when God made you to be great.* Sometimes there's a lot of Altitude in a few words. Your next move is in those words.

A MIRROR PARABLE

I don't usually like listening to TV preachers. They sound boring to me and it seems that they're going over the same stuff all the time. Usually if I come upon one, I'll just sort of click on by and get to *Paula Dean*—then I'll shift to MLB network to check some scores and see how my team is doing. It was interesting the other day when God said to me, *"Michael, go look in a mirror."* So, I went and looked in a mirror. God said,

"What do you see?" I was suddenly stuck in a mirror parable.

The next time I was watching TV, I hit upon a well known preacher guy. He starts by asking this question, it's a preacher guy kind-of question, *"How will God judge us?"* He then gave a brilliant answer by asking three more questions.

First, *How much light of truth did we know? Second, How much opportunity did we have? Third, What did we do with it?*

How much light of truth did we know means—How much do we know about the story? How much did we know about Jesus? How many of His words have we heard over the years? How many times have we been in church or how many times have we read the Bible; read Paul's letters; read the prophecies? How much light of truth did we know? What's the aggregate of truth in our lives?

How much opportunity did we have means— How many times were we in a moment when we could have embraced Him into our lives? How many times? Two times? A dozen times? Were we at a moment when we could have said, *"Yes. I believe."* Just like John believed in a moment in his life. Just like Paul believed in a moment in his life. Just like Mary believed in a moment in her life.

And finally, **What did we do with it means**—In other words, did we grab the moment? Did we mark that moment? Did we say, *"That's the truth that will define who I am and where I am going."* To know who you are and where you're going, you must know who Christ is and where He came from. And then you must make a move.

The thirst for God is still there. Why does the universe exist rather than nothing? How did humanity come to be on this remote blue speck of a planet? What happens to us after death?

THIRST

Recently I was at the airport trying to catch a flight to Charlotte and I met a friend who was catching the same flight. We were connecting in Charlotte but going to different places. The perfunctory announcement came overhead that all flights were canceled due to fog. An attendant asked that we all get in a line while they tried to work something out for each of us as best they could. That didn't sound good. We stood in the line and the line wasn't moving. We stood in line and talked some more and the line still was not moving.

Then we heard through the *line grapevine* that there was a strong possibility if we left the line and went downstairs we could possibly re-book ourselves and still get out of the airport. So, we said, let's be rebels. Let's be renegades. Let's be radical. Let's get out of this line that's going nowhere. Let's go back through security and go downstairs and try to re-book ourselves. So, we scurried back through the airport maze and got in another line when suddenly I got a phone call from the office saying that I was re-booked on another flight and I had to get to the gate ASAP as the flight was leaving in 30 minutes. Rebooking here I come. So, I went to the other airline, which will remain unnamed, because I don't want anyone to lose their job. Delta. When I got to the counter a pleasant person greeted me and I said, *"I've got to get on this flight to Chicago. It's leaving in half an hour."* She punched it in the computer, *"You're 2 minutes too late. You can't get on, it's after the 30 minute window."* I said, *"I have to get on the flight! Can we go talk to those other Delta folks over there? They look like they can handle an emergency like this."* She shrugged her shoulders and said, "Go ahead sir." I went over and talked to the other Delta folks and said, *"I've got to get on this flight. I have to get to Chicago for a meeting. I'm meeting a friend!"* And they looked at me and said, *"Well it's just too late, but we'll take a look at it."* I think they said that just to placate me. They checked the computer…it didn't work. They checked again…it didn't work. They checked again…it worked! All of a sudden a woman handed me a boarding pass and I'll never forget what she said, *"Run as you've never run before in your life!"* I stared at her and felt like saying, *Have you looked at me?*

But I had the boarding pass and so I started running, well sort of, I'm taking two steps at a time on the escalator! I set an escalator record. And then, I'm running and (this is the truest story I could ever tell you), there was a guy being pushed in a wheelchair. He's in my way! It was terrible and it was rude, but I sort of half jumped over him and kept going. I thought, *I'll apologize to him in heaven, I do not have time right now.* They pat me down. I grab my shoes. I don't even have time to put them on. I'm sprinting. I slide into the last gate. I'm out of breath. I handed my boarding pass to a woman and blurted, *"I'm here for the flight."* She shot back, *"The plane is still in Raleigh 200 miles away!"*

That is the story of our lives. We're scrambling. We're going places at the speed of escalators. We've got to get somewhere! We think we have a ticket. We think we know what we are doing. We think somehow what we've achieved in life is going to get us there. We think our tenure is going to get us there, our retirement is going to get us there. We have a ticket in hand. We think we have it all nailed down technologically or philosophically. Sometimes we even think we have it nailed down spiritually. But it's not *God's spirituality*, it's *our spirituality defined by our demands.* It's *our theology,* not *His theology.* We tell Him who He is. We're flying forward to the end of our lives on a wing and a feeble prayer. Don't miss life's greatest Altitude moment just because what you believed sounded good inside your head. You desperately need to know who He was and where He was from. This is important stuff! The thirst for God is still there. These questions must be answered. When you make a decision for Christ you are making a move that changes everything. You're not perfect—never will be—but you're gaining Altitude in new ways. You're making a decision that says *I know who I am because I know who You are. I know where I'm going because I know where You came from.*

> *You're not perfect—never will be—but you're gaining Altitude in new ways.*

Jesus predicted the future. He explained the universe was created by love. Now you know who you are. Now you know where you're going. Now you're not thirsty anymore. It's time to craft your soul.

LAST ALTITUDE STORY

During the Civil War, President Lincoln would attend New York Avenue Presbyterian Church, on Wednesday nights. The pastor, Dr. Gurley, allowed the President with his official aide to sit in the privacy of his study. The study door was open to the pulpit so they could hear the message, but not be a distraction to the people. One Wednesday evening, as Lincoln and his aide were walking back to the White House, the young man asked, "Well, what did you think of tonight's sermon?" Lincoln replied, "I thought it was well thought through, powerfully delivered, and very eloquent."

"Then you thought it was a great sermon?" the young man continued.

"No," Lincoln replied, "it failed. It failed because Dr. Gurley did not ask us to do something great."

Altitude is calling you to greatness.

The story of your next flight waits to be written. *Altitude is gained or lost from the sum of your moves, as you are answering two succinct questions.*

That statement tells the story of my life. It tells your story too.

Your next move changes everything.

Dear Michael,

My best friends are limpers. Gimpy people are my pride and joy. That's why you grow tired and weary of clumping along, Michael, it's because I want you to know who you are.

This limp I bestow upon men and women is one of the hardest parts of our relationship. Not many people expect it. The jolt of it sends some people reeling away from Me shouting about My unfairness and insensitivities. But they are always wrong. Your limp is your blessing and your new name comes from it. Few achieve much without the limp. It is the limp that forces you to understand the complexities of relationships. It implores you to answer the real questions of why you were born and what you should do. The limp gives texture and color to your days. It offers you insight into others who limp and may have something to teach you about the higher levels of Limpology.

You see it is those who limp who ultimately win, because they've won their game at the heart level. It's the limpers who maintain the greatest dignity, the limpers who build the strongest communities, the limpers who lead the best, the limpers who love the best. Gimpy people make My heart race for it is with them that I remind the world of the true meaning of grace. While many think grace is a free and restful experience, it's anything but.

If grace is vacant of sacrifice, it is not grace that you are seeing at all. Grace is given strength when you wrestle hard through the night toward a vision of self-sacrifice. When you embrace hardship and strained efforts, as the cost for changing the world, grace is most clearly present. If Christianity is just you keeping yourself happy and avoiding the wrestling match you'll never win anything. Songs of worship must need rise from sweaty hearts after all. This is how you know where you're going.

And so I go on through the centuries, giving out new names like Courageous, Humble, Broken and Servant to my limping crew. The best you can do is to be on My team of faller-downers. It's a good team to be on. Every sunrise illuminates a rag tag bunch dragging themselves onto a field called Faith. Gimpy people play better than you would think.

One Life. One Limp. Keep Moving. We Win.

Air Traffic Control

1. How did we get to the point where the message of Christianity has drifted so far from what Jesus taught, by His life and words?

_____

_____

_____

_____

_____

2. Which of the quotes hits you the hardest?

❏ Napoleon

❏ H. G. Wells

❏ Larry King

❏ Augustine

Explain why.

_____

_____

_____

_____

_____

3. Reflecting on Rocky Bleier's statement, where are you accepting *good* instead of *great*?

_____

_____

_____

_____

_____

4. If God views us through three lenses, how does He see you right now? Share briefly your story of thirst.

_____

_____

_____

_____

_____

5. How much light of truth did I know?

_____

_____

_____

_____

_____

6. How much opportunity did I have?

_____

_____

_____

7. What did I do with it?

_____

_____

_____

_____

_____

8. What will stick with you from this Altitude study five years from now?

_____

_____

_____

_____

_____

Flying Higher

Straw: Finding My Way, Darryl Strawberry, (HarperCollins)

A Resilient Life, Gordon MacDonald, (Thomas Nelson)

The Me I Want to Be: Becoming God's Best Version of Yourself, John Ortberg (Zondervan)

The Case for Christ: A Journalist's Personal Investigation of the Evidence for Jesus, Lee Strobel, (Zondervan)

The Case for Christ: The Film, Lee Strobel, (Zondervan)

Flight Log

My notes on Know Who You Are...Know Where You're Going

_____

_____

_____

_____

_____

_____

_____

_____

_____

_____

_____

_____

_____

_____

_____

_____

_____

_____

_____

_____

_____

_____

_____

Epilogue

Two other men,

both criminals, were also led out with him to be executed. When they came to the place called the Skull, there they crucified him, along with the criminals—one on his right, the other on his left. One of the criminals who hung there hurled insults at him: "Aren't you the Christ? Save yourself and us!" But the other criminal rebuked him. "Don't you fear God," he said, "since you are under the same sentence? We are punished justly, for we are getting what our deeds deserve. But this man has done nothing wrong." Then he said, "Jesus, remember me when you come into your kingdom." Jesus answered him, "I tell you the truth, today you will be with me in paradise."

Luke 23:32, 33, 39-43

BLOOD FLOWED STEADILY from his wrists twisted across his forearms and dripped to the ground. He summoned one more burst of energy, pushed himself off the balls of his feet, felt the pain shoot through his thighs, took a gulp of air mixed with sweat and survived another minute.

When he was a boy, his life had been a hell of emotional confusion. His father died when he was nine. People could see the grief in his eyes when he played in the alleys. They saw it tattooed across his face, a face that looked so much like the man who had given meaning to his life. The face of a child tells a story of truth. Busy adults rarely take time to read it.

Desperation drove him to the street when his mother was killed in a freak accident in the marketplace. There were no relatives to take him in. Not being Jewish he didn't fit into the one community that could be counted on to make sure no one fell through the cracks. He fell through. At twelve he was his own man losing himself in the street life and dark corners of Jerusalem's seedier areas. Prostitutes, thieves, and scam artists became his mother and father, his brothers and sisters. Never having learned to love, it was easy to learn self gratification by taking. Take what you want. Take what you need. Today a small score in the market. Tomorrow a mega heist from a Sadducee's home. In and out, watching the shadowy night fall. Knowing it was your friend, your comforter in a way of life guided by darkness.

Darkness always claims a human heart turned inward. He was a boy learning to play the game by men's rules. A contradiction in terms. He epitomized the paradox of evil being present in a world created by a loving God. His own concept of God, though weak, had not died out altogether. God was like the crumbs left after a meal. An afterthought. Something to be brushed away. Food for mice. How could this disjointed polytheistic faith of his youth ever mean anything when it was the hurt and pain that spoke so loudly? What drove the cacophony away, the gratification of the moment, the thrill of owning something that moments before belonged to another, had become the icon of his worship. And yet, if he searched his soul, which rarely he did, an emptiness remained. It had only been camouflaged for a moment and would have to be satiated again and again. His mind's voice haunted him. "Oh, pain that will not release the soul. Am I enslaved to eternal affliction? Will torment abide to death, perhaps beyond?"

Twisting his head before another deep breath, he caught sight of the King. It was a ghastly scene. People were cursing. One woman uttered enough profanity for ten men. Several soldiers stood a perfunctory guard while others gambled in back of three crosses. They were an odd group. These mercenaries, muscular and smelling of sweat soaked leather, talked about the money earned on this trip and about marrying and settling down in small towns outside of Rome. They kept it no secret that amongst themselves they thought Caesar and all political leaders to be poor examples of manhood. Real men exchanged sweat for bread. They faced danger head to head, not from a remote palace, while drinking wine and being entertained. Finally, to amuse themselves, they gambled for the King's humble raiment, laughing and carousing at the feet of this bloodied monarch. It was a scene that would not happen in any other kingdom except this one of darkness which would not know its royal guest who had so carefully wrapped himself in humanity. So he was dying with a king. Not bad for a common thief who last week had been caught in the house of one of the governing officials of Pilate's regime. He made his mistake and now paid for his sin with his life. It was that way. He accepted life on terms of the law of the street. An eye for an eye. His life for his sin.

The King remained in agony. Once He called out for water and was offered a vinegar infused sponge. Another time He said something to a woman who was apparently His Mother, as she stood by a young man in front of the crosses. In the early moments of the tortuous death sentence, it had been easy for him to hurl abuse at this defeated King along with everyone else, including his cohort in crime who symmetrically balanced the scene by hanging opposite the King. But now as darkness curtained the execution, an eerie silence froze the crowd. The wetness on his back turned cold in the wind. His flesh chilled. He was afraid of this night come in the middle of day like none other before. He began to think of his sordid years. What had he gained from all of the taking? What had been healed inside of him? The pain was ever there.

The King, in His entrenched misery, offered peace. He spoke of forgiveness for the executioners. It all happened so quickly as the soldiers walked toward him with heavy clubs to break his legs and bring death swiftly. Almost out of breath he blurted, "Jesus, remember me when you come into your Kingdom." On a faith that hung like a thin vapor between strands on a spider's web, he believed that somehow reaching out to the King would make a difference. It was a grand risk. Could a person receive what he doesn't deserve by a king's decree? Could a man be freed while dying on a cross?

He was emancipated as they smashed his legs and his body sagged. No more breath. No more pain. He was home and loved for the first time in a long time. A shell of a man hung on a cross outside of Jerusalem. No one saw the flicker of faith but the King and the angels. No one would ever know how eternity hung tenaciously to his last breath. And no one heard the ripping of a long thick curtain, as the grace of God rushed to soar over the whole earth.

Group Leader Appendix

SETTING UP YOUR ROOM

It's important to make your room as workable as you need it for your group. There are many types of rooms to work in. You may be in a classroom at a church or a family room in someone's home. Here are some ideas to help you have a great group experience:

1. Have soft music playing in the room as people come in (for ambience).

2. Have lighting that is soft and cozy for the room. If you're in a room with fluorescent lighting, think about bringing in some floor lamps.

3. Have extra pens/pencils available.

4. Refreshments are always good to have. Some basic snacks, mints and water can be a baseline to work with. Refreshment costs can be shared by group members or group members can rotate in bringing snacks.

5. People should be able to easily move into groups by turning their chairs around or by moving into adjacent spaces.

6. Having extra tissue boxes around and a supply of napkins on hand also meet a basic group need.

BOUNDARIES WITH GROUPS

Group work is rewarding in many ways, however, your group will always need you to lead, direct and guide. Here are some ideas to help you as a group leader/facilitator:

1. Talk about confidentiality at the first session.

2. Tell people how important it is to do the reading for each session, but if they don't get to it you still want them to come, because the group experience is important in and of itself.

3. Ask people to honor each other in the use of time.

4. If someone in the group is overly extroverted and uses extra time meet with them privately. Affirm their sharing but ask them to be sensitive to the group's need to have time to process.

5. If someone is introverted and doesn't talk you can ask them to share when there is a non-threatening question to gently get them in the game.

6. Tell your group you will keep time and keep them moving along.

7. Tell them you will be praying for them and they can call you with any group related concerns.

Let your group find its personality and grow. Leading a group is more of an art than anything else. If you feel it's time to move ahead, move ahead. If you sense giving them a few more minutes would be helpful, give them a few more minutes. Listen to your group and use good boundaries.

For excellent coaching refer to: *Making Small Groups Work: What Every Small Group Leader Needs to Know,* Henry Cloud & John Townsend, (Zondervan)

Connecting Flights

Willow Creek Association and The Global Leadership Summit
willowcreek.com

Cloud-Townsend Resources
Ultimate Leadership
cloudtownsend.com

Water 4
water4.org

ORPHANetwork
orphanetwork.org

Haiti Partners
haitipartners.org

Ken Davis
Dynamic Communicators Workshops and Seminars
kendavis.com

The Evangelical Association for the Promotion of Education
EAPE.org

mysongstosing.com
Parenthood. Life. Laughter.

Michael Simone
altitude@springbranch.org

Couples Who Pray
coupleswhopray.com

Paul Braoudakis, Editor
mvppaul@me.com

Notes

Introduction

1. Peter F. Drucker, druckerinstitute.com

Your First Move
Desperately Seeking Altitude

Epigraph
Lt. Col. Rob "Waldo" Waldman, *Never Fly Solo: Lead with Courage, Build Trusting Partnerships, and Reach New Heights in Business* (New York: McGraw Hill, 2010), 7.

1. Carlin Flora, *The Pursuit of Happiness* (Psychology Today, January 1, 2009)

2. Lt. Col. Rob "Waldo" Waldman, *Never Fly Solo: Lead with Courage, Build Trusting Partnerships, and Reach New Heights in Business* (New York: McGraw Hill, 2010), 7.

Your Second Move
Forgiveness is a Dirty Word

Epigraph
John Ortberg, *The Life You've Always Wanted* (Michigan: Zondervan, 1997, 2002), 129.

1. Carly Fiorina, *Tough Choices: A Memoir* (New York: Penguin Group, 2006)

2. Famous Proverb: from many sources

3. Shakespeare: William Shakespeare, *The Tempest*

4. Ephesians 2:8-9

5. Tony Blair, *A Journey: My Political Life* (New York: Knopf, 2010), 191.

6. Dr. Henry Cloud & Dr. John Townsend, *Boundaries Face to Face: How to Have That Difficult Conversation You've Been Avoiding* (Michigan: Zondervan, 2003), 71.

7. Jimmy Carter, *Sources of Strength* (New York: Times Books, 1997), 68-69.

8. M. Scott Peck, *Further Along the Road Less Traveled* (New York: Touchstone, 1993), 39-40.

9. Ibid, 46.

Your Third Move
Crash Course

Epigraph
Dag Hammarskjold: *Markings* (New York: Knopf, 1964), 213.

1. Dennis Overbye: *Physicists Find Elusive Particle Seen Key to Universe* (New York Times, July 4, 2012)

2. Brenning Manning, *The Furious Longing of God* (Colorado: Cook Communication, 2009), 129.

3. Richard Dawkins, *Man vs. God* (Wall Street Journal, September 12, 2009)

4. Karen Armstrong, *Man vs. God* (Wall Street Journal, September 12, 2009)

5. Three Dog Night: *Easy to Be Hard* (The Best of Three Dog Night, 1982)

Your Fourth Move
Shift the Sexual Vortex

Epigraph
Robert Burns, *A Red, Red Rose*, Scottish Poet, 1759-1796

1. Mark & Grace Driscoll, *Real Marriage: The Truth about Sex, Friendship, and Life Together* (Tennessee: Thomas Nelson, 2012), 112-113.

2. Joseph Stiglitz, *The Book of Jobs* (Vanity Fair, January 2012)

3. David Carr, *The Erotic Word: Sexuality, Spirituality and the Bible* (New York: Oxford University Press, 2003), 11.

Your Fifth Move
Seize Courage

Epigraph
Bill Hybels, *Courageous Leadership* (Michigan: Zondervan, 2002), 206-207.

1. Purim is a festive Jewish holiday that celebrates the deliverance of the Jews from their enemies in the biblical book of Esther. Purim is celebrated on the fourteenth day of the Hebrew month of Adar, which is usually in March. Purim is so-called because the villain of the story, Haman, cast the "pur" (the lot) against the Jews yet failed to destroy them. The Purim holiday is preceded by a minor fast, the Fast of Esther, which commemorates Esther's three days of fasting in preparation for her meeting with the king. The fast is then followed by two days of dancing, merrymaking, feasting and gladness where Jews celebrate by telling this story, drinking, giving gifts to the poor and food to each other. The primary commandment related to Purim is to hear the reading of the book of Esther.

Your Sixth Move
Gutsy Conversation

Epigraph
Thomas Moore, *The Bird Let Loose*, Irish Poet, 1779-1852

1. Albert Einstein, (New Jersey: Princeton University Press)

2. 2012 Global Leadership Summit presentation

3. Brenning Manning, *Souvenirs of Solitude* (Colorado: NavPress, 2009), 17.

4. Philip Yancey, *Not What It Seems* (Christianity Today, March 2007)

5. Philip Yancey, *Prayer: Does It Make Any Difference?* (Michigan: Zondervan, 2006), 267.

6. Water4 Foundation: water4.org

7. Philip Yancey, *Prayer: Does It Make Any Difference?* (Michigan: Zondervan, 2006), 267.

8. Ibid, 267-282.

Your Seventh Move
Answer the Right Questions

Epigraph
Joseph Brodsky, 25.XII.1993

1. Jackie Gingrich Cushman, *Christmas Joy I Can Believe In* (December 21, 2008)

2. Ibid.

3. Charles Wesley, *Hark! The Herald Angels Sing* (1739)

Your Eighth Move
Know Who You Are...Know Where You're Going

Epigraph
Anna Quindlen, *A Short Guide to a Happy Life* (New York: Random House, 2000), 10.

1. Michio Kaku, *Captain Michio and the World of Tomorrow* (The Wall Street Journal, March 9, 2012)

2. Ibid.

3. Tina Brown, *Holy Smoke! God save us from the godly* (Newsweek, April 9, 2012)

4. Ibid.

5. Andrew Sullivan, *The Forgotten Jesus* (Newsweek, April 9, 2012)

6. Tina Brown, *Holy Smoke! God save us from the godly* (Newsweek, April 9, 2012)

7. Andrew Sullivan, *The Forgotten Jesus* (Newsweek, April 9, 2012)

8. Napoléon Bonaparte, French Emperor, 1769-1821

9. H. G. Wells, British Author, 1866-1946

10. Larry King Interview

11. Augustine, 354-430

12. Bruce Larson, *What God Wants to Know: Finding Answers in God's Vital Questions* (HarperCollins), 46-47.

CPSIA information can be obtained at www.ICGtesting.com
Printed in the USA
BVOW031117171212

308269BV00001B/1/P